Basics First

Let Money Buy Happiness and a Central Store that Provides Essentials for All

T0154600

Basics First

Let Money Buy Happiness and a Central Store
that Provides Essentials for All

Sema Dube and Manu Dube

BOOKS

Winchester, UK
Washington, USA

First published by iff Books, 2017
iff Books is an imprint of John Hunt Publishing Ltd., Laurel House, Station Approach,
Alresford, Hants, SO24 9JH, UK
office1@jhpbooks.net
www.johnhuntpublishing.com
www.iff-books.com

For distributor details and how to order please visit the 'Ordering' section on our website.

Text copyright: Sema Dube and Manu Dube 2016

ISBN: 978 1 78535 589 9
978 1 78535 590 5 (ebook)
Library of Congress Control Number: 2016951899

A CIP catalogue record for this book is available from the British Library.

Design: Stuart Davies

Printed and bound by CPI Group (UK) Ltd, Croydon, CR0 4YY, UK

We operate a distinctive and ethical publishing philosophy in all
areas of our business, from our global network of authors to
production and worldwide distribution.

CONTENTS

Preface   1
1. Modeling Financial and Economic Systems   3
1.1 Fundamental Issues   4
1.2 Libertarians and Egalitarians   7
1.3 Outcomes   11
1.3.1 The good   11
1.3.2 The bad   12
1.3.3 The unknown   15
1.4 So What Now?   16

2. Revisiting Mr Crusoe   19
2.1 Wealth and Money   23
2.2 Key Considerations   25

3. The Crusoes   31

4. A Broader Socioeconomic System   35
4.1 Proposed System   36
4.1.1 Currency   37
4.1.2 Distribution of essentials   37
4.1.3 Currency-based transactions   37
4.1.4 Net money   38
4.1.5 Problems   38
4.1.6 Available money   39
4.2 Characteristics of the Available Money System   40
4.2.1 Stability of currency   40
4.2.2 Economic regulations   40
4.2.3 Wage restrictions and motivation to work   41
4.2.4 Government spending, taxes and inflation   42
4.2.5 Fairness of currency   43

4.2.6 Disparity   44

4.2.7 Efficiency and productivity   46

4.2.8 Observations and predictions   47

4.2.9 Policy decisions   48

4.2.10 Large investments   49

5. Resolving the Debates   50

5.1 Libertarians versus Egalitarians   50

5.2 Practicability of Free Markets   51

5.3 Impact of Technology   52

5.4 Cash versus In-kind Assistance   53

6. Conclusions   54

6.1 Comparison with Existing Systems   54

6.2 Foreign Trade   58

6.3 Starting towards the New System   60

Endnotes   62

References   65

To all our furry, feathered and finned friends
We owe you a gentler, happier world

Preface

Is it virtuous to work harder if there is not enough work? Can individuals be responsible for themselves if their fate is determined more by others' actions than their own? Where would self-improvement end when doctorates no longer offered protection against automation? Can we preserve jobs without discouraging innovation and restricting the free markets that have made our lives better? Soon we will have to answer these questions even as our complex financial and economic models are unable to predict effects of policies reliably. Policies which affect billions of lives.

Then there are the right-left debates. They have been going on for several hundred years and seem no closer to resolution today than when they started. The problem is that both sides have some aspects of the truth and miss other elements. Phoenix is north and west of Tucson. If you believed you had to go north to get there, you would not get there any sooner than "Go west, young man" would take you there. Computer models can actually make things worse. It is like having a supersonic jet. Depending on your north versus west beliefs you could end up in Canada or over the Pacific, farther away than when you started. As the race to prove one side right heated up, would anyone stop and ask if we even needed to go to Phoenix in the first place? We have to revisit the fundamentals of financial and socioeconomic systems to ask the most basic questions rather than complicate the situation more.

We explore the concept of money starting from what we can and cannot say about what an individual could want. Free markets, in a sense, consist of isolated individuals who make decisions for their own benefit in an environment that includes additional individuals. When individuals agree to be a part of a system, and such agreement is essential for maintaining a stable system, they agree to give up several freedoms. They agree to respect property rights and by doing so they give up the ability to exploit their natural environment freely. In return for such restrictions the system must provide them with some benefits. We do not need to assume that everyone wants to live solely to support others any more than everyone wants to spend all their time trying to earn more. Simply accepting that everyone would be happier if their own survival was made as easy as possible, and beyond that different people want different things, may be sufficient. Our results would show it is, and that it is possible to construct a simple financial system where no one is forced to do anything but it is in everyone's own interest that the essentials for survival are provided to all.

The analysis is easily accessible to non-specialists. It has to be. If we aim to describe decisions that people make consciously, it makes little sense to come up with a mathematical model most of us would not pretend to understand. It is we, after all, who supposedly carry out these analyses to make our conscious decisions.

No one can presume to have the final word on such a subject. Our main aim is to have the book be a seed for discussion where everyone can participate, by showing that it could be possible to change our systems for the better if we were to focus on the basics first. It would have been too painful to attempt, but for the good people at John Hunt who somehow made the dreary task of publishing the book a pleasure each step of the way.

1

Modeling Financial and Economic Systems

There are no known laws of nature that govern human behavior in the same sense as physical laws govern the motion of particles. This makes it difficult to model socioeconomic and financial systems mathematically. We can always find equations that explain past observations but it is increasingly clear that such models may not have predictive power.[1] If we did have a model that could predict the effects of policy decisions on the economy, would the Board of the Federal Reserve need to vote?

How can a model that explains the past be unable to predict the future? Consider a tribe for which rain is so important that it is a god. Why does it rain? The rain god is benevolent. Why did it not rain this time? The rain god must be angry. Ceremonies must be performed to propitiate him. What if it does not start to rain after the rituals? Perhaps something was missed. More intense ceremonies are now needed. Rain at this stage would only be a lesson to the tribe to treat their traditions with more respect. What if it still does not rain? The council of priests pronounces that the tribe has made the sun god unhappy and ceremonies are needed to correct that. No rain? The sun god and the rain god are fighting. Explanations and ceremonies keep changing till it begins to rain. When it does, as far as the tribe is concerned they not only explained why it had not rained, they even managed to fix the problem. Over time the pantheon expands and becomes a fundamental paradigm for all aspects of life. Life, after all, depends on rains.

A model that starts with an assumption that is not true does not get closer to reality as more complexities are added to explain increasing quantities of past data. It is over-fitting. This is not to argue that such models do not have any practical utility in giving us a sense of control over matters related to our survival. When all else fails, ceremonies to propitiate rain gods are still carried out in drought-hit areas across the world.

Our mathematical models for financial and other social systems may actually be one step worse. The tribe does not have to poll its members as to whether they believed it had rained in some imaginary place to decide if their model worked satisfactorily.

1.1 Fundamental Issues

The quantities we model are not physical values, and belief in models influences realized results. If everyone believes a model that predicts the stock price of a company to be $100, the stock price becomes $100. As the company releases new results it may turn out the stock price should have been different. We then refine parameter values based on the new data and may even add new explanatory variables. Calculating the simplest of parameters, like the β (beta) of a company which describes how its returns change with market returns, is not straightforward. If we use too short a period to measure the relationship the results would not be statistically significant. If we use too long a period the company itself could have changed over time as also the markets, which means the relationship would no longer be valid. At times we even introduce an explicit factor, how many historical values to use, and estimate this dynamically for estimating parameters to come up with a value that would give the best possible fit.[2] Models with parameters whose value can change depending on external conditions are especially difficult to validate because if they are complex enough we can always find parameter values that will fit a given set of observations.[3] In physical sciences we can run experiments under controlled conditions to guard against over-fitting. In economic and financial systems we do not have this luxury and depend on historically realized results. This brings us back to belief in models influencing realized outcomes. If we wish to look at more complex models, derivatives were meant to better manage risk. Borrowing from Keynes in a different context (Kuehn, 2013), we would suggest such models are "an extraordinary example of how, starting with a mistake, a remorseless logician can end up in Bedlam." Computers are the ultimate remorseless logicians. We believe their predictions at our own risk.

Agent-based simulations may provide an alternative but such simulations require that agents and the rules of the system be modeled properly. The basic idea is very simple. Instead of developing complex equations we simply assign individuals some properties, have them follow a set of rules, and run some simulations to see what kind of behaviors and results emerge. Swarm behavior became a popular venue for research when it was realized that extremely simple rules can lead to complex observed behavior, such as the v-shaped patterns migratory birds take up.

The problem, again, is that humans are not particles with simple equations that can describe their behavior. Modeling human agents involves the types of beliefs individuals may hold and how such beliefs form and evolve (Gargiulo and Huet, 2012; Kitto and Boschetti, 2013), their decision-making processes (Yukalov and Sornette, 2014) and their actions and their interactions with other agents in a manner that could be cooperative or competitive in varying measures (Brede, 2012; Schweitzer et al., 2013; Janssen et al., 2014). What constitutes successful behavior may change over time (Kampouridis et al., 2012). Individuals may have significant differences in their power and ability to effect change, and may even have different proclivities as to the extent to which they follow the rules of the game. The enforcement of rules is carried out by individuals and may not always be fair or uniform. The rules themselves are ultimately endogenous to the system. It is the emergent behavior of individuals that leads variously to meta-stable tribes, gangs, kingdoms, empires, nation-states and their alliances, each with its own rules. Such systems can evolve over centuries, or even collapse within days, based on internal and external impetuses. Agent behavior in a specific context, such as in financial markets, could be influenced by broader social, cultural and political systems and by rapidly changing technological regimes, along with individual psychological factors. In a sense the complexity is shifted to modeling agent behavior. If it were easy to define individual behavior and preferences *a priori*, or if it were sufficient to work with some averaged assumptions, would companies that provide all services for free in exchange for collecting massive quantities of detailed personal data about individuals have such high valuations?

Perhaps we are being over-dismissive. How can computerized trading be so widespread if we do not have any financial or economic models that can actually predict outcomes? Computers, after all, work on garbage-in garbage-out and any errors would lead to the wrong answer. The originator of computerized trading realized that he did not have to predict the correct stock price, if such a thing even existed, only the stock price large investors would calculate using their equations. As long as he could calculate this faster than the institutions whose calculations were not computerized, he could make a profit.[4] Today, when not every large institution uses the same formulas, we have front-running where servers co-located with exchanges get data a fraction of a second before others. Large and consistent profits are made via dark pools which allow a fraction of a cent profit based on orders already placed, multiplied by the large number of trades which are conducted at high frequency. It has little to do with technology facilitating free markets and better predictions, but rather using technology to exploit loopholes. Many major financial institutions survive only because they are too-big-to-fail.

1.2 Libertarians and Egalitarians

Model or no model, economic and financial decisions have to be made. In the absence of meaningful predictions from objective models we are forced to turn to philosophical arguments which are not necessarily better founded. Human evolution has led to the conflicting characteristics of compassion and competition, and both help with our survival. The corresponding philosophies of egalitarianism and libertarianism profess similar goals of enabling people to live happy, meaningful lives even as they prescribe divergent means to this end. Libertarians do not wish for productive individuals to limit themselves in terms of wealth generation or to be forced to work for free-riders. Egalitarians argue that concentration of resources could lead to owners of resources effectively being free-riders in perpetuity and so redistribution is essential. The commonality is the undesirability of forcing one to work disproportionately for benefiting another. The differences lie in what makes individuals happy and whose, and which, rights need to be protected (see for instance Bird, 2014; Gourevitch, 2014). This makes the viewpoints incompatible (Arnold, 2014). In other words the debates can never really reach a conclusion. They have been going on for several hundred years.

A related debate persists between systems with centralized control which rely more on cooperation, and free markets which promote competition.

Let us first show the basis for cooperation using a made-up example. Let us say you have a small piece of land where you grow some wheat and some vegetables. Your neighbor does the same. It is not very efficient; different crops need different conditions and some of the land is wasted in separating the wheat from the vegetables. If the two of you were to cooperate, one person could grow just wheat and the other just vegetables more efficiently. Then the two of you together would have more wheat and more vegetables than before. Imagine how much better things would be overall if everyone could cooperate together in this way. Mathematically, it is well known that global optimization over a domain dominates local optimizations over its sub-domains. Centrally planned economies should then outperform decentralized ones.

So why does it not work? Global optimization presumes a single global objective function whose maximization would be in the best interest of everybody. It means both of you like the same vegetables and both of you are happy if total production is increased. There are no issues with how much work each one of you have to put in, and how the total produce is distributed. It really is not easy to find such neighbors. If everyone were that understanding there would be no need to put up any system. In other words, walking shoulder to shoulder works great as long as everyone wants to go to the same place, along the same path, at the same speed, and is also happiest to have everyone else there with them. This does not hold across any large group of people over the long term. Individual objectives could, of course, temporarily become aligned under extreme circumstances. Your neighbor and you would probably be ready to join forces and defend yourselves against a group of outsiders trying to take over your land. Propaganda to convince everyone that they must work for some obscure common good, and ever-present external threats, become increasingly important for the continuing survival of such groups.

Free markets start by acknowledging that people are competitive. If everyone wants the best for themselves, it is not possible to have a central authority dictating what people should or should not do. After all, the central authority is also human and they will dictate what is in their own best interests. Their basic philosophy then becomes let people do what they want, and let them trade with each other without any restrictions. Sounds simple enough till you realize that lack of rules does not mean trade is free. In theory, one could simply take over someone else's goods and walk away if it was possible to get away with it. Worse, one could simply take over their resources and send them away. Ignoring this is ignoring the history of the world. So after we manage to acquire some property, one way or the other, we create rules for protecting it and set up common defenses. Will trade then be fair? Not necessarily. If one person owned some property upstream they could cut off your water supply. If you need water and do not have any, how much would you be willing to pay for it? Free trade means both parties come to the table without any compulsion and decide upon a mutually agreed value. A prerequisite is the absence of any threats to their survival. A negotiation with one party under the gun does not qualify as free trade.

So how do we ensure people are assured of their survival without placing any restrictions on economic activity? Everything is possible in theory, and so we take the easy way out. We simply assume that this happens. Magically.

Free-markets theory starts by assuming that everyone obtains their survival needs regardless of the happenings in the markets, characterized by "manna falling from heaven."[5] We can then prove mathematically that no one would be worse off, and at least one person would be better off. Of course it is reasonable that free trade applies to trading surplus goods against surplus wealth.

If manna were to fall from heaven no one would care for economics or finance. There is no way to separate economic activity that affects survival of individuals from that geared towards surplus or non-essential production. Restrictions on the former necessarily imply those on the latter. Once such restrictions are in place, an analysis of why the system fails to deliver degenerates to debates over whether the problem is free markets or the restrictions placed on them.

If the underlying assumption is not satisfied then it follows logically that we cannot conclude free markets are good for everyone. Supporters of free markets argue that if everyone worked hard for their own benefit, they would all somehow get enough to survive, and then after this state is achieved all trade would indeed be free. Without any proof as to whether this always will happen in the real world, it is simply kicking the can down farther. If producers are entirely free to set prices, an individual may be unable to support themselves if the prices set by the market are greater than what they can afford. Others could be forced to make unfair trades for their goods or labor to ensure survival, implying greater profits for those who already have a surplus. Those with greater wealth can also potentially tilt the playing field, such as by repealing labor-protection laws or legalizing front-running, which again increases disparity.[6] Assuming that compassion or personal charity can help satisfy the assumption is unrealistic, wealth not being positively correlated with compassion.[7]

Of course we can always kick the can a little farther down by assuming everyone can borrow unlimited quantities of money at zero cost. Reality again does not allow for this. Perhaps then people can borrow any small amount of money, at some interest, and start a business that will generate enough income to support them and pay back the lender? Perhaps not everyone has attempted to get a business loan.

Finally we can always try to kick the can sufficiently far into some undetermined future with the assumption, more likely the hope, that things will return to rationality and everyone who works hard will not just survive, but thrive. Survival in the meantime remains a day-to-day issue for many, and no one has yet survived the long term.

The failure of the most extreme form of central control has left free markets as the dominant philosophy, but that does not make it true. It does not necessarily make it false either. We have to look at the results we have obtained in the current situation where we are trying to implement free markets without dropping manna from heaven, amid accelerating technological developments.

1.3 Outcomes

We have to perform our own ceremonies the best we can determine how. With cheap and abundant computing power we are naturally inclined to use mathematical models to guide policy at various levels. Outcomes in terms of realized results have been mixed.

1.3.1 The good

We cannot deny the benefits that current socioeconomic systems have brought to our lives. Work is easier and safer, with drudgery and risk increasingly automated away. Doctors can look up the latest medical information and even patient records online from anywhere, and telemedicine and remote surgery provide access to world-class medical care in far-flung areas. Genetic medicine can literally absolve us of the sins of our forebears. Computers are better, faster and cheaper, as is access to online information. Coursework from the best universities is available online. We can browse vast libraries online, for free. Entertainment is endless and we can talk to people anywhere in the world instantaneously. We have polluted the planet along the way, but information technology is perhaps the first technology that can help us reverse environmental damage. It can make devices more efficient and facilitate use of alternative energy sources. Our cars and trucks will soon drive themselves, faster and more efficiently, without our intervention. Trains run without engineers and aircraft can fly themselves. This will remove human error, the single largest factor in most accidents, of course once errors in the codes and automation equipment have all been fixed. Virtual reality and telecommuting can make a significant proportion of travel redundant. Robots can farm, cook, serve the food and clean up afterwards. Cities and homes will be smart, perhaps smarter than us.

All of this has required large, global corporations with investors, researchers and workers across numerous countries and, equally importantly, financial and economic systems that could support such innovation and development. The critical factor here has been a positive reinforcement cycle. As computers got better, they became more useful, which meant increased sales volumes. Economies of scale then helped make them even better and also cheaper, which in turn increased sales even more. This is why a bulk-produced $100 cell phone today is more capable than a custom-designed million-dollar computer of a few decades back. You can hold the cell phone in your hand and even drop it without any problems. If you entered the air-conditioned building needed to house the old computer wearing dirty shoes, it could break down. The air conditioning, of course, was needed for the computer and was not intended for user comfort.

1.3.2 The bad

It is with increased application of computers to areas such as finance and economics that the lack of reliable models resurfaces with a vengeance. Markets now are a complex jumble of competing algorithms, not all of which can be right, and whose implications even their creators may not always understand.[8] The ability to move large quantities of money globally, and instruments such as derivatives, can make markets more volatile. There are increasing worries about a potential perennial drought for the many who are unable to placate the rain god whatever ceremony they perform. Perhaps the concerns are misplaced, but it does not hurt to check.

Over-reliance on models with questionable assumptions, along with the unintended consequences of regulations pertaining to credit-rating procedures and electronic registration of property titles, led to the 2008 financial crisis. In the US 2.6 million jobs were lost and there was significant underemployment, making it the worst year for employment since the

Second World War (Goldman, 2009). The International Labor Organization (2013) reports that high global youth unemployment may lead to a lost generation, "scarred" with respect to future earnings, which distrusts socioeconomic and political systems even within the EU. Youth unemployment in 2012–2013 was 12.6% globally, 18.1% in developed economies and the EU, 28.3% in the Middle East, and 23.7% in North Africa. Even in developed countries measurable detrimental effects on the well-being of populations are accumulating, such as on lifetime expectancies for those at the lower end of the educational spectrum in the US[9] and on health and life-expectancy in Greece[10] where austerity measures to tide over the crisis have slashed public assistance.

Increasing the skill-level of the population does not always help. In Turkey, which has one of the fastest-growing information and communications technology sectors, the number of universities has more than doubled in less than a decade and an increasing number of students who complete primary schooling go on to complete either university degrees or higher vocational schools instead of entering the workforce at intermediate levels. Even as more people with higher degrees are employed, there are also more unemployed people with higher degrees (see Dube et al., 2015). The latter may be worse off as they have invested time and resources in obtaining higher education and do not have anything to show for it. Student loans are a major issue (see, for instance, El-Erian, 2015) in the US where automation is increasing in high-skill technical areas (e.g. Frank, 2012) such as finance (e.g. Son, 2016) and engineering, even in computer science with codes automatically writing codes. In countries such as India, even as software has become the largest private sector employer, postings for a few government jobs which require primary education elicit millions of applications including tens of thousands from those holding higher degrees all the way up to doctorates (Rahman, 2015). An oversupply of institutions can also impact the quality of education, and increased duration of education does not always translate into higher skills but rather is a means for delaying entry into an already overcrowded job-market. As Singh (2014) notes, in India a PhD may be the easiest degree to get. Even in developed countries standards may have to be relaxed to fill seats (e.g. Sieniuc, 2014). There are open jobs, but employers typically complain there are not enough candidates with the right skills. The right skills, of course, change rapidly with advancements in technology. The answer has been lifelong learning, which has been promoted across the EU as part of various programs. Bulut (2010) points out that the model can also be viewed as learning-unto-death where employers are only too happy to transfer what would normally be on-the-job learning, to outside vocational training that is employee responsibility and is often taxpayer subsidized.

Governments have been experimenting with centralized versus free-market economies; strong and weak currencies; high, low and even negative interest rates; promotion of financial innovation versus taxing high-frequency trading or restricting short sales; various levels of public support; high expenditures versus austerity; and with promoting development of labor-force skills and educational levels as well as businesses.

The wealth disparity in a majority of countries is growing. A total of 62 richest individuals in 2016 have as much wealth as the bottom half of all humanity. This compares to 80 in 2014 and 388 in 2010, even as the population has grown by 400 million over the same period. The richest 1% own more than the remaining 99% combined, with the share of the lower 80% being 5.5% (PTI, 2014; AFP, 2015; Elliot, 2016). A total of 147 companies control 40% of the world's resources with 737 companies controlling 80% (Upbin, 2011). Jaumotte and Buitron (2015) refer to Berg and Ostry (2011), Berg et al. (2012) and OECD (2014) to argue that higher concentration can lead to slower growth. About one in nine, or 795 million, individuals face undernourishment (FAO, 2015). The number has been decreasing but this has required significant government intervention, from providing more assistance to removing stifling regulations. One in six individuals in the US receives food assistance, the number rising to one in two if additional programs such as those for medical assistance are included (USDA, 2015). The Food Security Act of India (The Gazette of India, 2013) aims to cover two-thirds of the population (Government of India, 2013). Such schemes can be wasteful, and in India it has been estimated that only 27% of the expenditures reach the intended beneficiaries (Sukhtankar, 2012). Fluctuations in food prices led to 51 food riots in 37 countries in 2007–2014, with insufficient attention being paid to the potential for unrest due to shortages (World Bank Group, 2014). There is some evidence that price fluctuations due to currency volatility typically hurt those at the lower end of the wealth spectrum more (Cravino and Levchenko, 2015). Debates persist on all aspects of such assistance, from whether it is affordable or even appropriate to provide assistance to those in need,[11] whether the assistance should be in cash or kind,[12] to what constitutes need.[13]

1.3.3 *The unknown*

Where will information and communications technology (ICT) lead us? We do not even know where technology itself will be a few decades from now. While technology has advanced tremendously, in many cases exceeding early expectations, it has not made "[u]nemployment...disappear from the face of the earth forever" (Licklider and Taylor, 1968). Proponents of technology argue that it provides workers with more free time, with any increase in unemployment being rent-seeking behavior (e.g. Mabry and Sharplin, 1986), and that there is a positive relationship between technology, wages and high skills (e.g. Katz and Murphy, 1992; Doms et al., 1997; Goldin and Katz, 1998; and Caselli, 1999).[14] Other researchers suggest that the impact of new technologies on unemployment and salaries is realized over longer time periods as the workforce gets retrained (Mincer and Danninger, 2000) and that technology reduces low-skilled jobs but allows lower-skilled workers to perform high-skill occupations (Dobbs et al., 2012). Others, still, argue that technology potentially leads to substitution of labor (Mokyr, 1990), increase in disparity (e.g. Forestier et al., 2002) and chronic unemployment (e.g. Frank, 2012). For developing markets, Sassi and Goaied (2013) suggest a joint relationship between ICT diffusion, financial development and economic growth in that the benefits of financial development may accrue only after a certain threshold of ICT development has been reached. In India, implementation of ICT projects for poverty reduction has not been uniformly successful (Mehta and Kalra, 2006). Similar to the case for business systems where it has been argued that results depend on how such tools are used (e.g. Ceccobelli et al., 2012), researchers have also argued that while it is not necessarily inherently skill-complementary, ICT could be made so by design (e.g. Acemoglu, 1998). There may be merit in all of these arguments. As in other areas, we do not have definitive answers in scientific literature, and arguments as to the effect of technology in general on disparity and employment have also been ongoing for hundreds of years. The difference now is that rapid developments have made change happen much faster.

1.4 So What Now?

It is not that society in general is unaware of the problems. We all face them every day. If centralized control does not work, why not just make sure the assumption underlying free markets is met by providing everyone with the survival requirements? Communities are increasingly considering experimenting with forms of basic income guarantees. Concerns about such schemes relate to how to pay for such schemes. Government schemes are always under stress during economic downturns when revenues are low and such assistance is especially important. If the required goods are in short supply, giving everyone more money would simply lead to inflation. Then there is also the issue of why take money from people who work for it and give it to those who do nothing. Would it not motivate the latter to continue not doing anything? The last concern demonstrates the issues vis-à-vis the theory of free markets and their practical interpretations. The first is that free markets assume that manna falls from heaven and do not require individuals to work under threat to their survival. The second is that if, as is assumed for rational individuals, everyone were competitive and wished to maximize their wealth, there is no reason anyone would simply stop at the basic handout and not use their spare time to gain even more wealth. Perhaps rational individuals wishing to maximize their wealth is not a reasonable principle for broad socioeconomic systems?

We explore a simple system that allows for universal support without the various objections raised against basic income guarantee schemes. The key is to align the self-interest of individuals with providing essentials to the group. What it requires is a look at the fundamental assumptions regarding individual behavior and the concept of money.

It is increasingly being realized that how money is created and lent is a key factor in the situations we face today. There are moves in Iceland to curb the out-of-control financial markets that created havoc with their reliance on complex models, and the financial institutions which utilized these. There are sovereign money initiatives in Switzerland (see, for instance, Bershidsky, 2015). There are demands in the US to audit the Federal Reserve. Even recent IMF research papers (e.g. Benes and Kumhof, 2012), which, though, are by no means official IMF policy, discuss alternatives such as the Chicago plan. The IMF recently has been increasingly vocal about the issues related to disparity and the negative effects of austerity, something that is rather surprising.

Then there are always those who would rather return to gold.

Instead of trying to continue within existing paradigms we look at the issue *de novo*. We consider simple systems first and then only change what must be changed as systems get more complex. In businesses, processes and procedures sometimes get needlessly complex because of the historical path the business followed, and technology can allow for business process re-engineering to drastically simplify matters. We suggest applying financial re-engineering to the problem and removing any extraneous assumptions or procedures to help simplify the system and keep the financial system focused on the basic goals of its underlying socioeconomic system. The first step, of course, is to determine the appropriate goals.

2

Revisiting Mr Crusoe

Billions of individuals and tens of thousands of computers now interact in financial and economic systems. Individuals are driven by their own goals. The computers that participate in the system are agents for individuals who have programmed them to achieve their goals. What goals drive individuals?

Let us consider an isolated individual, i. They are perfectly free to do whatever they wish and there is no one to save them from the consequences of their actions. The individual must, first and foremost, attempt to ensure their immediate survival. This is a basic physical instinct. Nothing else would be relevant if the individual were to not survive at least for the time being.

Let q_{id} represent the quantity of goods the individual must acquire or produce for daily survival on day d. If they could obtain x_{id} units of goods per hour, the time to obtain the required goods for that day would be q_{id}/x_{id} hours. It depends on the available resources, the skills of the individual, and their current condition. The surplus time available to them that day would be

$$w_{id} = 24 - q_{id}/x_{id}$$

$$...(2.1)$$

We consider daily values because of the natural diurnal cycle, and because a few days would represent a reasonable time-frame where a person could not survive without food and water. Barring emergencies, the time needed must include the time to recover for the effort to be sustainable.

The total surplus time an individual has over their lifetime, which starts at day $d = 0$, up to $d = Z_i$, where Z_i is the first day their daily surplus time becomes negative, is

$$W_i = (24 - q_{i0}/x_{i0}) + (24 - q_{i1}/x_{i1}) + \ldots + (24 - q_{iZi}/x_{iZi})$$

$$\ldots(2.2)$$

We assume that if the surplus time were negative on a particular day, the individual could not survive beyond that day because they could not obtain their requirements for that day within 24 hours. Such an individual cannot simply work harder to survive. An individual with zero surplus time can just maintain survival. They have no time to pursue any other aim.

An individual with positive surplus time could spend it as they pleased. If the individual were reasonably rational they would understand that there could be times when they may not be able to produce anything. They may also be aware of seasonal variations where certain resources may not be available during certain times. To mitigate such risks individuals could trade off some of their current surplus time for future surpluses. They could *save* by using the surplus time today to produce extra and store it to reduce future requirements. They could also *invest* their surplus time in increasing their productivity to reduce the time required for obtaining the essentials in the future, such as by exploring their surroundings to obtain additional resources or increasing their skills and abilities.

How would someone decide on how much time to spend saving and how much to invest? Working extra to save may require more essentials to fuel the effort and more time for recuperation, although to an extent it may also increase the physical capacity of the individual and could be an implicit investment as well. Depending on the type of work involved, it may also lead to faster degradation of available resources. If some goods were perishable it would not help to simply produce more of them. Some time would need to be invested in finding ways to prolong shelf life. Even if the environment were such that working longer would always generate a net positive of essentials and goods were not perishable, working till you drop and starting again on waking up may not necessarily be the most effective strategy because investing time in improving productivity could increase the surplus even more. On the other hand investing without any savings would at best result in potentially 24 hours a day of surplus time, but then even the most efficient individual may temporarily be unable to produce anything. Investments require resources as well, and are risky in that returns are not guaranteed.

If they were highly rational the individual could look at the opportunities available, and for each such opportunity the expected returns and what they expect to be the risks. They would also consider their risk aversion. It would be even better if they could quantify all that, and then all they would need to do would be to plug the numbers in and find the optimal course of action.

The question remains though: optimal to what end? Rationality extends to finding an optimal solution given the objective function, not necessarily to defining the objective function. We have to describe what individuals do, not what we may think they ought to do.

Can we assume that an individual would like to maximize their expected lifetime? Immediate survival is certainly a strong driving force, and perhaps experiencing seasonal variations would make survival over a year or so equally critical. Survival 10 or 20 years down the line does not have the same immediacy. Individuals may place different values on spare time now versus expected lifetime.

While we cannot say what an individual would like to do with their surplus time, we can assume that all other things being equal no one would like to spend more time working towards their survival. This is not the same as individuals attempting to maximize their spare time. Mathematically it is a partial differential condition and not an absolute maximization. The quantity of spare time can be traded off against what the individual could do in their spare time, or its utility to them. One person could prefer to spend more time working simply to be able to survive if it allowed them to live by the sea and they strongly preferred that to living in a forest. However, given that they were living by the sea, they would prefer needing to spend less time ensuring basic survival, than more. The more free time they had, the more they could save, invest or surf. Individuals may also place a different value on spare time today versus that in the future. Overall they will wish to maximize the expected utility of their spare time, but each utility function will be personal.

We could come up with a general equation for each day where the individual sets aside some time to obtain survival essentials, some for savings, some time to invest, and has some free time they would wish to consume for some other activity. They would also decide whether they wish to consume any saved surplus. The next day the savings and productivity will be a function of the history of their prior decisions, and they will again make production, investment and consumption decisions for that day. We could give weight to the free time on each particular day in proportion to the utility of free time on that day. Then we could try to optimize the course of action an individual should take to maximize their utility over their lifetime.

One problem is that the weighting factors that denote how much utility the individual places on free time, when, would be completely up to the individual. Since we cannot specify such factors on our own, we cannot really determine the optimal course of action for an individual *a priori*. We could always make some assumptions, but then the results will be only as good as what we assume.

The second issue in describing actual outcomes is to what extent individuals would indeed prefer to spend time carrying out such analyses. Most individuals would probably make decisions somewhere between knee-jerk reactions and long-term planning for the future over their entire lifetime. All future values, including utility factors, are expectations. What makes individuals happy changes with time, as does what individuals think will make them happy in the future. Expectations also change based on the realized results of prior actions, whether such inferences be statistically valid or not. Even for a rational individual the optimal level of analysis would depend on past experience in terms of how stable the environment has been, and whether past expectations have been a good guide for subsequently realized outcomes. The optimal level of analysis would also depend on individual ability, and we cannot make assumptions about this any more than we can make assumptions about individual preferences.

Predicting what an arbitrary, isolated individual would do is reasonably difficult to say the least. We can assume they would try to ensure their immediate survival and beyond that they would do whatever made them happiest as compared to other alternatives available to them, and that all other things being the same they would be happier if they had to spend less time ensuring their basic survival rather than more. To predict anything specific we would need to know their skills and experience, their psychological state, their physical condition, their preferences, and details of their environment.

In the best possible case for any individual, manna would fall from heaven and they would have 24 hours of surplus time a day, leaving them free to do whatever else they wished.

2.1 Wealth and Money

Roughly speaking, wealth is something that individuals would like more of, something they could use to save or invest at present for increasing it in the future, and something they could consume or expend to meet any other goals they might have. One contributing factor to wealth would be the resources available to the individual. If they lived in areas with plentiful essentials, obviously they would be better off than living in areas where survival was difficult. Another factor is their own skills and abilities. An individual with better relevant skills and abilities could get more out of a given set of resources or could figure out how to do so. Can we combine these various factors into a single measure?

For an isolated individual, we suggest their *wealth* is their *surplus time*. It incorporates the combined effect of the resources available to the individual, their skills, and their physical and mental states. Available free time is the most fundamental resource for any activity an isolated individual may wish to undertake. It is also naturally limited to 24 hours a day.

Money, in terms of currency, is irrelevant to an isolated individual. However, in general it is something we can use universally to exchange for goods without having to work for producing them. In this sense money is the savings of stored essentials. It is not a measure of wealth, but represents wealth, which is spare time, that has been stored in the sense that it was used to create savings. The time thus spent can be recovered when the individual consumes the saved surplus instead of producing an equivalent quantity.

Why do we not take surplus time to be money or stored surplus goods to be wealth? If there are no goods available to exchange, money has no value. In the absence of stored essentials an individual would still need to work to obtain these regardless of how easy or difficult it was to do so. Wealth is a broader concept. If an individual were to live in an area where simply collecting the produce of local trees and plants within an hour would provide them with sufficient survival essentials for the day, and they had saved two days' worth of essentials, they would have two units of money. If they lived in an area where obtaining the essentials took eight hours instead, they would also have two units of money if they had two days' worth of saved essentials. Unless the individual preferred the second case for some other reason, they would be better off in the first case than under the second one because they have more spare time, 23 hours versus 16 hours. They could invest the additional time, use it to generate savings at a greater rate, or use it to achieve some other personal goal. They would be wealthier.

In such an economy individuals are responsible for themselves. The system is also fair in that an individual consumes over their lifetime what they produce. The only problem is that an individual cannot start to satisfy their basic needs till they have reached a certain age. If left isolated on the very first day, the lifetime would be zero, as would be the wealth.

2.2 Key Considerations

It is important to consider isolated individuals, especially for free markets where each participant can still be thought of as an individual making decisions for themselves in an environment that also includes additional individuals.

We can see that to be able to survive individuals must have sufficient time, given their current skill-levels and the available resources. They must also have spare time if they are to be able to save or to invest in improving their skills. This does not change if individuals were to come together to form a system. The poor are not always free to work harder to survive or improve their situation if they cannot survive, or can barely do so, in their present circumstances. The presence of other individuals can even make it harder to survive because not all resources and all possible courses of action are available to everyone.

Surplus time is one factor that combines the effects of the skills of the individual, how they use the skills, and the resources available to them. It is something individuals would like more of and something that is a basic resource needed to work towards any other objectives they may have. It is like the wealth of an individual. There is evidence that even in existing systems people are happier if they try to maximize their available time and not their money (Mogilner, 2010). At the same time while money does not lead to greater happiness it does reduce sadness, perhaps because it reduces the stress related to everyday issues such as getting a leaking roof fixed.

We cannot define personal objectives in terms of what individuals should do with their spare time. We cannot assume all individuals are rational in the sense that they would want to achieve the same goals as the individual carrying out the modeling, and different individuals also have different abilities. This is a critical issue if the system contains multiple individuals.

Individuals would still like to maximize the utility of their wealth, not their wealth *per se*. The formulation for the utility of wealth involves several other factors. One common factor of course is any risk to immediate survival, which is an instinctive motivation. Other than that, it includes personal preferences, and increasing wealth will not necessarily increase its utility if other factors are impacted negatively. With multiple individuals, the range of options only increases. Some people like to live in large cities where the living costs are higher; others prefer rural locations with cheaper costs of living. Even oil executives try to stop fracking in their own backyards (e.g. Woodyard, 2014).

The assumption that individuals wish to maximize their wealth instead of its utility could be problematic. If everyone were to be a disciplined investor in free markets trying to maximize their wealth, there would be no need for non-essentials unless their consumption directly helped the individual obtain even greater wealth. This could reduce investment opportunities for non-essentials and could then decrease wealth for those who have invested in such products or their marketing. At the government level this is reflected in attempts to impose austerity and promote growth at the same time. The resulting instability makes even survival difficult for many individuals.

Individual preferences also include whether or not to carry

out any long-term analyses. There is some evidence that individuals make decisions instinctively and employ reasoning subsequently to justify such decisions. Advertising is, after all, often deployed to prevent buyer remorse. While cheaper computing has made calculations easier and more accessible, our models still can only explain the past. Decisions often have to be made in real time. If, in our distant past, one were to come across a charging predator it would not likely have helped to set up explicit probabilistic equations and then solve them to come up with the best option. In existing systems high-frequency trading is based less on long-term predictions of how particular events will play out but rather on simple heuristic algorithms, perhaps employing some artificial intelligence, to estimate market movements fractions of seconds in the future. Such systems are not always stable, which puts into question the value of long-term analyses. Individuals who had analyzed their own observations of their parents and grandparents, had saved up for retirement, and were expecting pensions are increasingly finding this out. Individuals who have invested time, effort and resources getting trained in fields they thought would prosper, such as petroleum engineering, often find later on that fossil fuels are no longer liked, that technological developments have opened up renewable resources, or that geopolitical considerations have made new explorations and developments uneconomical. Borrowing against future income is not always a rational choice.

The usefulness of analyses based on long-term expectations depends on how fast the environment changes. With technological advancements change has been extremely rapid. The rate of change would argue against a system based on complex models for long-term predictions, but rather a simple system that reflects the results of all actions, as and when they accrue, so that individuals can better discern cause and effect.

Then we have the concept of money, which is a medium of

exchange that can be used to obtain desired goods within a reasonable period of time. This implies the presence of goods that can be exchanged and their desirability. Let us assume you have an apple orchard. You give 10 apples to your friend who grows pears, and get 15 pears in return. This would be barter. What if you did not want pears but bananas? You could give your friend the apples and get a note from them saying the bearer of the note will get 15 pears from them. You can then take the note to people who have banana plantations and see if they wanted any pears and how many bananas they would be willing to give in return. If both parties agree on two dozen bananas for 15 pears, you get the bananas and the plantation owner gets pears and your friend gets apples. Everyone is happier because in the end everyone got what they wanted. The note in this case acted like currency. The issuer of the note promised to give something, in this case, pears. To be able to make good on the promise the issuer has to have the pears. The note should be redeemable. Additionally, for the note to have any value, there must be someone in the group that liked pears and had something else desirable to provide in return. The best possible case would be if the note could promise something universally desirable.

In a larger system where different individuals have different preferences, survival essentials are precisely the goods which would continue to be universally desirable. Even as money can be used to buy different goods, the reason everyone would be happy to get money in exchange for their goods or services would be that they could always exchange it for survival essentials.

There is another consideration here, that of time. When would the bearer of a note wish to redeem it?

If a note is written backed by existing goods, a delay in redeeming it is not necessarily in the interest of the issuer because maintaining the goods in storage is costly. Similarly, redeeming the note immediately is not always better for the bearer because if they wanted the goods for future consumption they would need to store the goods instead of the issuer. If your friend wanted apples today, but you wanted the pears in return a year from now and your friend already had the pears, you could either get them now and store them yourself or you could have your friend keep them for a year. What if the pears got spoiled, or stolen from your friend's storage?

On the other hand if the note is not backed by existing goods but based on the assumption of the issuer that they would be able to obtain such goods by the time the note would be redeemed, there could be times when the issuer may not be able to procure such goods, making the transaction risky for the bearer. We cannot always simply state that a note promising to provide 15 pears one year from now is necessarily worth less than one promising to provide 15 pears immediately, or more for that matter.

The best approach that could be taken would be for the issuer to provide all information as to their storage status, the number of notes outstanding, the goods in storage, and their productive capacity, and let bearers and potential bearers decide based on their personal needs what value they would place on the notes and when they would wish to redeem them.

Currency is not a measure of wealth although the two are closely related. In existing systems we use monetary values to denote the value of wealth in addition to acting as currency, and assume that wealth maximization translates to maximizing its money equivalent. This is not always reasonable, especially if the value of money itself changes. Countries have removed several zeros from their currency without anyone becoming poorer, and hyperinflation has added several zeros to currencies without anyone getting richer. Governments also spend substantial effort adjusting the values of their currencies relative to others, an additional complication that must be incorporated in models. The fact that there are problems with fiat currencies does not suggest a return to gold either. The quantity of gold available with a group has nothing to do with quantity of available goods. There is some evidence that prices of basic items tend to be constant in terms of gold over the long term but such relationships break down during crises. Gold may have had value as currency in the past as it is a relatively rare metal that does not degrade. These qualities are no longer relevant in the digital age where numbers in accounts have as much permanence. They also cannot be simply carried away physically via theft.

The best possible case for any individual, that of manna falling from heaven, happens to be an underlying assumption for markets to remain free. This shows the severity of the assumption and that it must be dealt with explicitly.

3

The Crusoes

Of necessity an individual at times has to be dependent on others, and in turn has to have dependents at other times. The biological family is a natural unit that makes such interdependence feasible. Before we move on to more complex systems, we consider whether we need to add anything in the framework of isolated families.

Let us assume all adults in a family carry out the same tasks, with the same productivity, so that dependents may be divided among them equally. If individual i works towards securing the goods and services necessary for survival, and on day d has n_{id} dependents including themselves, each of whom require q_{id} as the daily minimum goods and services required for survival; and has an hourly productivity x_{id}, their daily wealth, w_{id}, is

$$w_{id} = 24 - n_{id}q_{id}/x_{id}$$

...(3.1)

If the total number of working adults be n_w, the total wealth of workers in the family would be $n_w w_{id}$. The limit of zero wealth again represents a sink boundary, implying that for a surviving family this quantity must be non-negative. The risk to survival is mitigated, though, in that in case of temporary inability of an individual to work, the load may be picked up by another. The total daily wealth of the family unit, including the dependents, supported by individual i is

$$w_{fid} = n_{id}(24 - q_{id}/x_{id})$$

...(3.2)

31

and again, with n_w workers the total wealth of the entire family would be $w_{fd} = n_w w_{fid}$. This includes surplus time children may have to invest in learning, and surplus time available for the elderly to care for, and train, children.

If a_1 represents the age, in days, when an individual starts to work and a_2 be the first day of retirement, their total wealth over a lifetime of a_3 days is given by

$$W_i = 24(a_3 - a_2 + a_1) + \sum_{d=a_1}^{a_2}\left(24 - \frac{n_{id}q_{id}}{x_{id}}\right) = 24a_3 - \sum_{d=a_1}^{a_2}\frac{n_{id}q_{id}}{x_{id}}$$

$$...(3.3)$$

The first term represents the 24 hours per day of surplus time during childhood and retirement where individuals do not have to work. The second term is the sum of the daily surplus times, starting the day individuals begin working and up until the day they retire. Assuming savings to be constant, so that individuals on average consume the daily requirements acquired, the net essential goods consumed by an individual for survival relative to those produced for themselves and their dependents are

$$Q_i = \sum_{d=0}^{a_3} q_{id} - \sum_{d=a_1}^{a_2} n_{id}q_{id}$$

$$...(3.4)$$

If we assume that the daily requirements for goods and quantities remain constant, for a fair system the difference between the goods consumed and produced should be zero, or

$$\frac{1}{n_i} = \frac{a_2 - a_1}{a_3}$$

$$...(3.5)$$

If the average lifetime be 80 years and each person could support one dependent in addition to themselves, so that $n_i = 2$, and $1/n_i = \frac{1}{2}$, the individual would have to work half of their life. For instance individuals could start to work when they are 20 years old and stop working at 60, so they would have to work half their lifetime. The dependent will switch over time from a child to a retired parent, and the person who supports the individual can switch from a parent during their childhood, to a child in their retirement. For a stable population, we assume that the family interchanges one child with another family via marriage at the appropriate age and in turn gains a spouse for the child retained. Each family of two adults (2P) will start working at 20, and will also have two children (2C). At this time, the grandparents (2G) will be 40, and will start supporting the great-grandparents (2GGP) who will have turned 60 and retired. The working individuals, 2P and 2G, will support 2C and 2GG, implying one additional dependent per working person on average. After 20 years, the 2GG will pass on, and the 2G will enter retirement and will be supported by the 2P who are now 40. The children, 2C, will start to work but there will also be two grandchildren (2GC) who will need to be supported, again implying that 2P and 2C will now support 2GP and 2GC, or one additional dependent per working individual, besides themselves.

The system is sustainable if population were to remain fixed. It is fair. Individuals in the family unit produce and consume the same quantity of goods that they would need to, for survival, if they had the same lifespan as isolated individuals. It is preferable as it allows for nonzero lifetime and wealth. Multiple workers also mitigate the risk of temporary individual inability to produce, such as due to sickness, and can lead to greater productivity with specialization.

Natural family affinity implies there is no need to enforce fairness explicitly, nor is there any need for explicit record-keeping as to contribution to production of essentials and their consumption. The total spare time represents the wealth of the family, and the savings are again equivalent to money. As for the case of the isolated individual, in the best possible case manna will fall from heaven and each individual can avail themselves of 24 hours a day of surplus time. What they would do with the time would be up to them.

There is no reason, or perhaps even any means, to enforce isolation of individual families, although small, closely knit, tribal communities could reach a relatively stable state under isolation and continue on for millennia in remote areas, acting pretty much as extended families in line with the analyses for single families. Money, or currency, would still be stored essentials. The wealth of individuals would still be their surplus time. What members of the group would wish for is that the environment be such that it makes the task of obtaining the essentials easier. At best, again, manna would fall from heaven.

Still there would be differences. More workers in the tribe could help tide over temporary inability to work for certain members, reducing the risk to survival. Division of labor and specialization may be more feasible and may lead to greater efficiency, although again questions of fairness and who has to work relatively more for their tasks would arise. A system would also have rules that restrict individuals. This starts to bring up questions as to whether individuals can be held responsible for their situation when their options are restricted by the rules of their group.

4

A Broader Socioeconomic System

There is no rule that keeps various tribes in isolation. The history of the world is proof of that. We must be able to deal with broader systems. As groups get larger there is no biological drive to support unrelated individuals, and competition would be present within the group along with compassion. What would be the characteristics of a system that could encourage various, disparate individuals to participate in it voluntarily?

Isolated individuals provide the baseline relative to which society restricts behavior. Society also provides additional choices, such as aircraft for flying which require cooperative action to design and build and would likely not be developed by someone who has never had contact with others. A *good* system would minimize the loss of choices relative to the case of isolated individuals, while maximizing the additional choices made available to individuals due to the cooperative actions of its members. For a group to be internally stable, members must believe that the trade-off is sufficiently close to their optimal point that the effort required for change would not be worth the expected benefits. Comparisons could be difficult, though, as different groups restrict different liberties and add different choices. The competitive nature of individuals requires attention to *fairness* which we restrict to an individual getting back from the group over their lifetime whatever they produced for it. A perception of unfairness could lead to discontent. Fairness is also subjective to an extent. Issues here could relate to resource ownership and what would constitute fair wages for work. Simply assuming market wages to be fair is not necessarily satisfactory if the underlying assumption of everyone obtaining their survival needs does not hold. This can have significant implications for the stability of the system.

Trade-offs may be involved between *good* and *fair*. A system that restricted everyone to producing and consuming a quantity *x* of goods would be fair. Another system could allow individuals to produce any quantity of goods they wished, provided they shared ½ of everything above *x* for distribution to those who could not produce enough to support themselves. The second system is *better* for those who could produce above *x* because they could always produce only *x* and simulate the first system; however, it would not necessarily be *fair* for them. Which system made people happier would depend on their individual preferences. We cannot decide such issues *a priori*.

4.1 Proposed System

We now start to explore a system that provides the survival essentials to everyone, thereby maintaining free trade for any surplus essentials or non-essential items. The goal is to satisfy the sole commonality it is feasible to find among the goals of isolated individuals, that of obtaining the requirements for survival in the minimum possible time. We wish to do so without placing restrictions on economic activities to be compliant with free-market assumptions.

The first requirement is for sufficient resources to produce the essentials for the entire group, without which it would be physically impossible for the assumption to be maintained. The question as to whether a group with sufficient resources will do so in the absence of economic regulations is a different issue.

We also assume that scientific consensus can be reached as to the daily quantity of various required essentials.[15] Let q denote such a bundle of the daily quantity of various essential goods, in the correct proportion, that an individual needs for survival.

We introduce a central store for the system. It can receive, store and distribute essentials to individuals. Any individual can deposit bundles of essentials, in the correct proportion, in the store. The central store does not violate free-markets principles as no one is required to provide essentials to the store. The store also maintains an electronic account for each individual which is used for currency transactions.

4.1.1 Currency

The quantity q of daily essentials is assigned a currency value of 1Π. Currency is generated and deposited into an individual's electronic account when they deposit essentials in the store. If an individual deposited m units of the quantity q of essential goods in the central store, their account is credited with the amount $m\,\Pi$.

4.1.2 Distribution of essentials

Periodically the central store distributes, to each individual, the quantity of essentials that would suffice till the next distribution. If the distribution is daily, each individual is provided with q units. If the distribution were monthly, each individual would be provided with nq units, where n is the number of days in the month. Each time n units of quantity q of essentials is distributed to an individual, their account is debited by $n\,\Pi$. Accounts are allowed to become negative in this transaction. The system keeps track of the total contribution to the store versus the total receipts from the store.

4.1.3 Currency-based transactions

An individual with a positive account balance can transfer currency from their account to any other account, in return for any goods and services. Such goods and services are obtained in the marketplace, outside of the central store system. An individual with a negative balance cannot transfer any money out, but they can receive currency in exchange for any goods or services they provide to others. Individuals are not required to use the central store currency for their transactions. There is no price control for any exchange of goods and services, whether via barter or using currency. Insofar as one individual may not be able to produce all components of the required bundle, creating complete bundles for the central store would also require trading in the marketplace.

4.1.4 Net money

The surplus essentials available with the central store, Sq, correspond to the net money in the system, S, given by

$$S = P - N$$

$$...(4.1)$$

where P is the sum over all positive accounts and N is the magnitude of the sum over all accounts with a negative balance. It is not possible to exchange 1Π per $1q$ of essentials for the total of the money in positive-balance accounts.

4.1.5 Problems

If we wish to keep the value of the currency fixed in terms of certain goods, it should be redeemable at its face value. The central store cannot do this as the available surplus matches the net money, S, not the total positive balance, P, that individuals could wish to redeem. If the central store were to redeem the available surplus at q goods per Π, keeping the price constant, the surplus would go to zero, while $P - S = N$ worth of positive currency, equal to the magnitude of the total over negative accounts, would remain in the system without any goods in the central store to back them up. Whether or not there are other goods in the markets that would maintain the value of currency is not under the control of the central store.

The money chasing goods in the marketplace increases with N, implying that some producers may benefit if not everyone is able to support themselves. Producers may also have an incentive to retain their surplus and release small quantities into the marketplace to keep prices above $1\Pi/q$. A higher price for surplus in the marketplace would provide incentive to divert essentials from the store to the marketplace. This would entail expensive policing. Hoarding, artificial shortages, and black-marketing in terms of illegal diversion of goods from a public distribution system to the markets are not unknown under existing systems either. The central store could freeze all currency transactions if available essentials were insufficient for distribution. It would create a stop-and-go economy. At the same time individuals with large negative balances would have little motivation to go back to work because anything they earned as currency would go towards reducing their negative balances.

4.1.6 Available money

We could reduce the complexity considerably by making a simple modification to the system. If A be the account balance of the individual after adjusting for the distribution for the next n days, the beginning available money in the account, A_f for the following n days is given by

$$A_f = \left(\frac{S}{P}\right)A = \left(\frac{S}{S+N}\right)A$$

...(4.2)

Here $<A>$ equals A if $A > 0$, 0 otherwise. During the next n days, each individual is free to use the available money in their account as currency, such as transferring it to any other account in exchange for any goods or services, or to redeem it by obtaining surplus from the central store at the rate of q units of goods per Π. Any currency the individual receives in exchange for any goods and services also remains available for use till the next time the available money is calculated. During the n-day period, available money acts like normal currency. Individuals can deposit essentials and get available money in their account at $1\Pi/q$, or they could withdraw surplus at the same rate. The total account balance changes the same way. Essentially the central store restricts the usable fraction of the currency at any time, based on existing conditions, and allows only redeemable currency to be used for any transactions. If individuals did not wish to be subjected to such restrictions they could always retain their surplus and store it on their own.

4.2 Characteristics of the Available Money System

The system would appear to ameliorate the various issues associated with universal provision of survival essentials within free-market systems.

4.2.1 Stability of currency

The total available money at the beginning is $(S/P)P = S\ \Pi$. It equals the surplus of Sq units of essentials available with the central store. If an individual were to withdraw essentials from the central store, the corresponding quantity of available money ceases to exist in the system. If an individual were to provide essentials to the central store, the corresponding quantity of available currency is added to the system. Parity is maintained in all cases. Any other currency transaction changes neither the total quantity of available currency nor the quantity of surplus in the central store. The central store can always redeem the available currency at the fixed rate of q units of essentials for 1Π.

4.2.2 Economic regulations

The system does not allow for black-marketing of essentials. If the current surplus be Sq units, providing an additional q units of essentials to the central store provides the producer with 1Π. If instead the same essentials were to be placed on the market, the total available money chasing the $(S+1)q$ units of essentials along with any non-essential items would still be $S \Pi$. Velocity of money is irrelevant here. Purchasers have a certain amount of available currency. They can redeem all of it at the central store for $1q$ of essentials per Π. No one then needs to pay more than $1q$ per Π for surplus essentials and there are no opportunities to profit by diverting essentials from the store to the markets.

What if producers wanted to sell components of the bundle of essentials individually on the markets? With sale and purchase prices of essentials from the store remaining fixed, market prices for components of essentials are automatically bounded. It would not be sensible to purchase a component of the bundle for greater than 1Π when 1Π of currency could be used to obtain the entire bundle of essentials from the central store. No price controls are needed on any component of the surplus.

If the central store has zero surplus left, all currency transactions are frozen automatically as there is no available currency in any account. The decrease in the available currency is gradual, with 1Π being removed each time a quantity q of essential goods is withdrawn. Assuming that society has sufficient resources to produce a surplus, there is always motivation to produce it or risk being reduced to barter. For a complex society barter is not easy, which is why currency is needed in the first place. Creating artificial shortages does not help for price gouging, as available money decreases accordingly and it is always redeemable. No restrictions on economic activity need to be applied or monitored.

Markets would still exist. Individuals could trade goods to create bundles of essentials in the required proportion that could be accepted by the store, along with any leftover goods as well as non-essentials. Individuals could also freely trade their labor for any goods or obtain goods via barter.

4.2.3 Wage restrictions and motivation to work

Those with negative account balances start with zero available money, but can spend what they earn before available balance recomputation to obtain any non-essential, or surplus, goods or services. They have motivation to continue working. At the same time there is no need to impose any restrictions on wages. Workers are not forced to work because of risk to survival. If they do not find the work sufficiently rewarding they can always choose to not work. Market forces can operate freely to fix wages. Individuals can also volunteer for the benefit of society without having to depend on employment for maintaining survival.

4.2.4 Government spending, taxes and inflation

Government expenditures with regard to provision of the essentials themselves are not an issue as the store creates the currency in exchange for surplus essentials while maintaining parity between the stored surplus and the available money. There are no inflationary issues with regard to essentials as their price is fixed automatically, bounded from above by the redemption value of the quantity q of essentials for 1Π.

Taxes would still be needed for creating and maintaining infrastructure for storage and distribution of essentials, as well as for essential services such as medical care and defense. The central store itself has no resources of its own. A simple scheme would be that if T be the amount of tax revenues that need to be spent over the next n-day period, before the recomputation of available balance taxes to the total of $T\ \Pi$ would be deducted proportionately from each account with a positive balance and be paid to the destination accounts. After this step, available money can be computed for all accounts as before.

We suggest taxes based on total positive balance because this represents the benefit the individual has been able to obtain, in terms of stored wealth, by being part of the society. The alternative of taxing transactions would require tracking them. This would be difficult for barters that are off of the central store system and would require expensive physical tracking. Holding of redeemable currency across periods imposes costs on the system. These costs are also related to universal provision of essentials to maintain the stability of the system. In India, for instance, there are lawsuits to force the government to distribute stored goods to those in need in case of famine or drought. Insofar as taxes go towards this, those holding the currency bear the cost.

Development of technology and infrastructure for more efficient collection, storage, and distribution reduces the associated taxes over time by making these more efficient and reducing maintenance costs. Individuals, including those with negative balances, could volunteer for some of the services and contribute by reducing the tax burden.

Could individuals reduce taxes by shifting money to accounts where the net balance is negative, such as their children's accounts which will be negative till they reach working age or simply as charitable donations to those with negative accounts? They could. Such transactions are also possible in existing systems which have tax-free charitable donations and tax exemptions for children. By doing so they would be providing to individuals with negative balances the ability to spend during the remainder of that period. Any money not spent within the period from the destination account will not be accessible because negative balance accounts are frozen each time available balances are recomputed. Even this would be beneficial as it would free up more money for everyone by reducing N. Spending is also encouraged for those with positive balances because if individuals were to hold on to the money, a portion of the money would be taxed.

4.2.5 Fairness of currency

For those who provide a certain quantity of goods to the central store, or those who create something else equivalent in value, the frozen portion of the money is not confiscated. It is just not redeemable for the next period. Consider an individual with a positive balance Q_i. If they do not provide any additional surplus or trade any goods or services for currency, and assuming the factor (S/P) remains constant, starting from the initial period $k = 0$ where they could spend $(S/P)Q_i$, in the kth period they are able to spend $(1 - S/P)^k(S/P)Q_i$. In other words, over time the individual can still spend virtually all the money they earned by contributing any surplus. The price of the essentials at the central store remains constant so they can always obtain the same quantity of essentials, or other goods of equivalent value, they produced. In this sense the currency is a fair store of value. The taxes, though, go towards the cost of creating and maintaining infrastructure for distributing them. If stored surplus were to be wasted, such as via spoilage, the quantity of available currency would be reduced automatically.

If the money is spent in a way that increases the factor for available money, the fraction that could be spent at any time would become greater. If society in general uses the money in such a way that the factor increases to 1, everyone who has contributed a surplus can spend it anytime, or can get back the entire surplus they provided to the central store. The system aligns the self-interest of individuals with ensuring that everyone has opportunities to produce the equivalent of at least what they need to survive.

4.2.6 Disparity

Since everyone obtains the essentials for survival and those unemployed have the whole day free to do whatever interests them, disparity is measured by N which indicates the overall level of those who cannot support themselves. In the proposed system an increase in disparity, defined thus, decreases the available cash for everyone in proportion to their account balance. The impact in terms of currency units is greater for those with more money. The key here is not that the currency is redeemable, as not everyone would wish to redeem it for essentials immediately, but whether it is transferable for obtaining other goods and services on the markets. The rich, if they wish to be able to spend more, have an incentive to reduce disparity out of self-interest. Similarly producers, if they wish for their customers to have more spendable money, have the same interest. The money however is only frozen, not confiscated, and the currency is not unfair to producers. As shown in Figure 1, the decline in available money with increasing disparity is especially steep as disparity increases from a small value, suggesting the importance of not starting on the path. If someone with a positive balance and someone with a negative balance could both offer a service for 1Π, it would be better for society in general if the person with a negative balance were selected because either it would be spent anyway, or it would increase the available cash for everyone in the next cycle, implying that consumers would have more money for purchase of goods provided by producers. It is not in the interest of producers to simply reduce the workforce to increase profits.

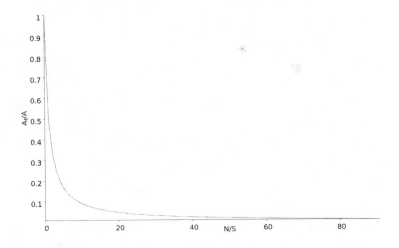

Figure 1: Impact of Disparity, *N*, on Fraction of Money Available, A_f/A, for Surplus *S*

Assuming that an individual with a positive account balance takes an action that maintained their account as positive, and both S and N change due to the action of all individuals including the one under consideration, the change in their available money after the next recomputation would be given by

$$dA_f = \left(\frac{S}{S+N}\right)dA + A\frac{N}{(S+N)^2}dS - A\frac{S}{(S+N)^2}dN$$

...(4.3)

The first term represents the change in the account balance, adjusted for disparity. The second represents a reward for increasing the surplus. It is also proportional to the account balance, suggesting that those with more money have a proportionately greater interest in increasing the surplus with the store or in supporting such actions. The third term is a penalty for increasing disparity and is also proportional to the account balance.

4.2.7 Efficiency and productivity

The system continues to promote efficiency and productivity provided the resulting gains are sufficient to offset the negative impacts of such actions. From Eq. (4.3), an individual would be at least indifferent to, if not supportive of, a transaction conducted by others which would not change their total account balance, as long as the increment in surplus, dS, at least equaled $(S/N)dN$. Thus, individuals could support actions that increased disparity provided the actions increased the surplus with the central store. The required increment in surplus is proportional to the current surplus. If society already has a large surplus, it does not help to increase the surplus marginally while placing individuals out of work. On the other hand if the surplus is small, it may help to increase the surplus, such as by mechanized farming, even if it means some individuals will end up being out of work.

The penalty is steepest for actions which only transfer wealth from the poor to the rich, more so if the actions also reduce available surplus. The penalty is on everyone as each transaction has two sides. If society in general supported such actions on balance, such as buying goods from individuals who impose a heavy social cost on the system while reducing prices somewhat, then the net of all actions would imply a penalty on the group as a whole. Of course if individuals believed that an action with temporary short-term pain would lead to long-term gains, they could still support it. The system can help with this.

4.2.8 Observations and predictions

Instead of operating on expectations and predictions of complex models the system automatically incorporates the results of actions, as and when they accrue, at the end of each recomputation period. Adjustments related to available money are made transparently, and based on present circumstances using known and unambiguously measurable values of the available surplus and account balances. There is no need to predict the future or obtain expected values, or to look at the past to estimate any parameters.

If fired workers find more profitable employment elsewhere, and it is often argued that it is better to release workers to the market where they could be employed more productively than to retain them and keep production inefficient, the corresponding benefits become available to society automatically. If they remain unemployed, the penalty will continue to increase as time passes. If after some time they find more profitable employment, benefits will again start to accrue. The entire historical impact is incorporated automatically.

Immediate and objective feedback via available currency directly impacts all group members and helps everyone realize the true costs and benefits of actions and policies, providing clearer cause-and-effect relationships. Such learning can be more beneficial for future decision-making. The system also removes complexities related to the value of the currency.

4.2.9 Policy decisions

The group will have to decide how frequently to distribute the essentials. This would determine the quantity to be distributed. Furthermore, instead of distributing to everyone on the same day, the group could distribute to different regions on different days. The optimal policy would try to minimize distribution costs.

Any time a distribution is made, the available balance must be recomputed across the system. However, the group could choose to recompute the available balance more frequently. Variations in the recomputation period will allow some leeway to the group in setting monetary policy to influence economic activity in the group.

In the limit of recomputation after each currency transaction, those with negative balances are unable to spend anything as each time they place money in their account, unless the total is positive, the available money at the next instant becomes zero. Such a system would be restrictive to those with negative balances in terms of currency usage and would also incur greater computational costs. At the same time those with positive balances can spend, or try to redeem, their entire balance in a sequence of transactions almost instantaneously. Of course if everyone with a positive balance were to simultaneously try to redeem their entire balance in exchange for surplus from the central store, after the first step was handled for everyone, the total surplus and the available money would go to zero.

Another decision the group needs to make would be the storage capacity of the central store. Greater storage implies greater money, but storage itself is costly. Given seasonality, a year's worth of storage should be the minimum. The limit would be the shelf life of the goods in storage less the time it took for an item to be consumed after leaving storage. Even if the group were to follow a first-in first-out policy, if the storage were full and distribution were to be made from the earliest arriving goods, these should still be usable. Any excess goods would be rejected by the store.

The system directs policy away from wasteful half-measures. In countries such as India the government may procure grains at support prices and provide income to farmers, but the stored grains then rot (Headlines Today Bureau, 2011). This does not increase the wealth of the group. The Π-based system focuses attention on storage because spoiled essentials make the equivalent currency cease to exist. The system requires that essentials be provided to individuals. Measures such as allowing beverage plants in certain areas to provide better employment in terms of higher wages, which ultimately lead to shortages of water and eventually lead to the plant being shut down, are also ultimately wasteful (AFP, 2014). The true costs of such endeavors would be apparent earlier under the system because local residents would need to be provided with such essentials by the central store on a regular basis.

4.2.10 Large investments

How would individuals pay for large purchases such as land or factories? If they had sufficient total money, but insufficient available money, they could always pay in installments. Such an approach may limit artificial property bubbles that otherwise arise in existing systems. Companies could be formed and could open a commercial account. It would be no different from personal accounts in terms of taxes and available money except that no periodic distributions of essentials would be made for such an account and thus it would not be subjected to the relevant reductions.

5

Resolving the Debates

One significant implication of the system would be that numerous long-standing debates would be moot.

5.1 Libertarians versus Egalitarians

An individual can choose not to participate in the system by simply returning the surplus they were provided, back to the central store, and maintaining a zero balance. They would not pay any taxes. They could use barter to trade goods and services or even come up with their own private currency. They would still have to abide by other rules of the system such as traffic rules or property rights, but even libertarians uphold such rules. No one is forced to work for free-riders. Insofar as libertarians do not wish to impinge upon individual economic freedoms, the freedom to not participate in the central store system but still trade with others by mutual agreement makes it free of any objections.

If an individual did not wish to obtain the universal assistance or pay taxes, but wanted to use the central store currency for convenience, they could do so as well. All they would need to ensure is to return their account balance to zero before each calculation period so that they do not incur any taxes or do not have any account balance frozen. This does impinge somewhat upon their liberties, but currency is a characteristic of an organized system and maintaining the system incurs costs, in turn imposing certain obligations on users. The cost of maintaining stored items to allow the currency to be redeemed increases as the currency is held for longer periods of time.

Everyone who wishes to participate obtains the essentials for survival automatically. Those who work are not bound to do so under threat of survival, so they do not have to accede to work conditions that they may consider unfair. Individuals are also free to provide volunteer services, or to simply donate to others if they so wished, without risking their own survival. It is not in the interest of society in general, especially those with more money as well as producers, to simply automate away jobs *en masse* to try to gain marginal profits. The more individuals are unable to support themselves, the more available money will decrease in proportion to the account balances for those with positive accounts, even as the value of the currency remains constant in terms of essential goods.

For egalitarians the level of services to be provided universally, such as medical or educational, would still be up for discussion. Technology could make provision of such services cheaper over time. University coursework is already available online, for free, and computers and internet access are also not difficult to obtain. Individuals can always find sufficient free time to educate themselves. Education for critical areas such as medicine could be provided free of charge in public institutions in exchange for volunteer service for a certain number of years upon graduation, offsetting the costs via reduced taxes. If people wish to benefit from options arising out of egalitarian ideals, they should also support the continuation of such programs. Those who do not wish to avail themselves of subsidized education in return for volunteer work for some time could opt for private institutions.

5.2 Practicability of Free Markets

The system is designed to enforce the basic assumption underlying free markets, one that ensures all trades are conducted freely, without imposing restrictions on economic activity. It bypasses the debate in existing systems as to whether markets without economic restrictions can remain free in a sustainable manner in the presence of increasing disparity.

The general principle is that if a system has external assumptions, there is no guarantee these will be satisfied. In order to ensure the system can continue to function, such assumptions should be bootstrapped so that the system can be isolated from the external environment. In this case the assumption of universal provision of essentials is bootstrapped using the assumption that a currency exists and that individuals would prefer to have more of it available for immediate use, than less.

5.3 Impact of Technology

The system makes available, in a sense, the true benefits of technology as workers who are replaced by automation can use their spare time to improve their skills rather than taking up lower-paid jobs to maintain survival which may not leave them time for other activities. Technological development would also help reduce taxes over time with better infrastructure and storage that does not need frequent maintenance.

The system does not place any limits on innovation. It does not prejudge the results, which are reflected in the available money as and when they accrue. Innovation which simply leads to transfer of wealth from those at the lower end of the spectrum to the higher end, without an equivalent benefit to the entire group in general, reduces the available money for everyone. Under free markets, society in general has no obligation to support such innovation.

While it would seem reasonable that under free markets individuals could choose not to accept innovation that ultimately harms them, this aspect could be somewhat contentious because the system discourages economies of scale for such changes when perhaps in the future they could lead to greater innovations. We suggest that if society could be convinced that such temporary pain leads to a clear path for future benefits, individuals could support such innovations. Under the system people can better track what was anticipated versus the overall realized outcome.

We suggest this approach is better. It makes little sense for people to be able to get a cheaper cell phone with many new features, but not be able to call for medical assistance because they could not afford it.

5.4 Cash versus In-kind Assistance

The system makes such debate moot because it allows individuals to decide the form of assistance for themselves. The default is assistance in kind because it is the goods that are required for survival. However, an individual who receives such assistance can always provide it back to the central store after the recomputation and obtain equivalent available cash in return, which they can use fully till the next recomputation.

In existing systems the issue is complex because providing cash assistance could increase inflation. It is possible for the prices of essentials to fluctuate. Essential goods may be in short supply. The Food Safety Act of India allows for providing cash if essentials are in short supply, although it is not clear how such assistance could help individuals to survive if required goods were not available or were too expensive. The available money system maintains a constant price for essentials and provides society with a direct motivation to ensure sufficient goods are available in the central store for distribution.

6

Conclusions

So there we have it, a system that does not impose any restrictions on economic activity and still allows for universal provision of essentials, making the benefits of free markets available to all.

6.1 Comparison with Existing Systems

Currency and distribution issues are significant factors which cannot be left as external assumptions in markets, and the system requires us to define a currency and some rules for it. Which system does not? The available money system is no worse than existing systems which need to depend on varied and conflicting predictions from complex models, voting, and attempts to manipulate the value of the currency against others based on anticipations of how it would affect the economy along with endless debates around these. It uses simple and transparent rules that do not require predicting the future. It automatically incorporates the results of all actions as and when they accrue while keeping the value of the currency fixed relative to essential goods. It leaves production and consumption decisions to figure themselves out in the context of a stable currency while ensuring everyone survives, and everyone knows the net results of the actions of a group as a whole.

An apparent drawback of the Π-based currency is that currency is generated only when a unit of surplus essentials is stored in the central store and all other goods are valued in terms of this currency. The total currency does not increase if society keeps the total stored essentials the same, but additionally produces cars or aircraft. Gold has been the traditional currency for millennia, and up until 1971 the US dollar (USD) was partially pegged to gold. The total quantity of above-ground gold has increased over time but the total quantity of gold is also necessarily limited, and is close to gold presently above ground (Erb and Harvey, 2013). The Π-based currency is digital, and so is as imperishable as gold while being easier to transfer. The currency cannot be stolen or carried away via war as transactions are only between accounts controlled by the central store. It obviates the need to mine gold other than for industrial purposes, which artificially places value on an otherwise useless activity. An increase in total money is possible with the new currency but requires the creation and storage of additional surplus essentials, which is inherently of value. Technologies that allow for digital currencies and long-term storage of essentials obviate the need for using gold as a relatively rare and imperishable intermediary for record-keeping. Technology cannot change the amount of gold present on earth, and if it could, gold would simply lose its value as money, but it can help with production and long-term storage of essentials. The move to connect USD with oil may be a natural evolution of currencies in that petroleum provides energy and compounds that are essential for the creation and distribution of essentials. However, the price of oil in USD varies significantly, oil itself may be environmentally unfriendly, and technology could reduce the need for oil-dependence. Connecting currency to the stored output, regardless of what was used to produce it, may be the next step. From a fundamental point of view money must be a means for an individual to obtain something of value in return. The goods that are desirable across individuals would be those essential for survival, and the stored surplus of these naturally represents stored surplus wealth against which currency can be issued.

The current system maintains absolute parity between the quantity of surplus essentials and the available currency at all times. The long-term stability of prices in terms of gold for essential goods and services, such as the price of a loaf of bread and the salary of a Roman centurion versus that of a US Army captain have been remarkably constant over two thousand years (*Ibid.*), which suggests such stability of basic goods in terms of currency is not impractical in the long term. Such relationships between gold and essentials break down in the short term, especially under conditions of hyperinflation and shortages, as owning a certain quantity of gold is no guarantee that the desired goods and services exist, and predicting the price others would wish to pay for the gold is not necessarily easy. The Π-based currency enforces price stability by definition and guarantees the availability of surplus essentials corresponding to the available money at all times.

Psychological benefits of nominal-value inflation aside, the absolute quantity of currency is typically irrelevant, with countries having added and deleted several zeros from their denominations without anyone getting richer or poorer. The Π-based currency is not unreasonable. It requires a person to be able to survive on 1Π per day, not that different from individuals surviving on $1 a day which was valid as a poverty estimate till the 1990s. In comparison with gold, taking the total value of above-ground gold to be $9 trillion (*Ibid.*) and using 9 billion as the global population, 9 trillion Π would translate to a stored surplus of 1000 days, which is less than three years. A 1000-day stored supply of goods for a country such as India would lead to a currency of 1.2 trillion Π, which would not require an abnormal velocity of money for a nominal GDP of approximately 2 trillion USD. Given that agriculture is seasonal and also varies from year to year depending on the vagaries of the rain gods, such storage capacity is not impracticable or unreasonable from a risk-aversion point of view.

Studies suggest it is more economical to simply provide individuals with essentials rather than bear the cost of individuals not having access to these, that such programs work better if there are no means tests, and that universal distribution programs are more acceptable politically. The proposed system is consistent with these observations.

There is no need for large bureaucracies, not even a revenue service, as taxes are calculated and withheld automatically. The expenditures are towards maintaining storage and distribution, essential medical services and defense, and any specific programs that the group members approve. All the tax collected goes directly to the destination accounts of those who provide such services.

People can choose not to participate in the central store system if they so wish, and at the same time they are free to volunteer and donate to others. No one is forced to work simply to be able to survive. The system provides more freedom than individuals simply being required to desire economic liberty and wealth maximization, as they have an option to do something else with their time. Both libertarian and egalitarian concerns are alleviated.

Innovation, if it helps the society, is automatically promoted as individuals can see the benefits in available money. Changes that end up being simply transfers of wealth from the poor to the rich penalize everyone in proportion to their money. Companies that simply fire workers for increasing their profits may lead to social costs. There are two sides to every transaction and if individuals buy the cheaper products from such companies they support such actions. However, there could be benefits as well. Each action cannot really be studied in isolation as it is the net result that matters. If fired workers can find more gainful employment elsewhere, forcing the first company to retain them makes no sense. The system does not prejudge results. It simply reflects the results in available money as and when such costs or benefits are realized. Those with more money and thus greater power are impacted proportionately more.

There are no restrictions on what companies can or cannot do in terms of wages and labor-protection laws. Consumers not buying from companies, if it is in line with their own self-interest, does not contradict free-markets philosophy and neither does workers not undertaking work if they consider working conditions exploitative. Employers who cannot find a sufficient number of workers at the wages they wish to offer are free to change their business model. They can also hire and fire as they please.

6.2 Foreign Trade

Could the system trade with other systems? For a group on a Π-based currency, the key would be maintaining parity of available currency with available surplus. If another system used the same goods in the same proportion, but the total quantity were different, then currencies would be convertible directly. For instance if a group used $2q$ as the daily requirements that were distributed and used a currency Π^*, we would have $\Pi^* = 2\Pi$. Other than that, the currency cannot maintain parity with fiat currencies, gold-based currencies, or currencies backed by some other mix of goods.

One possibility would be that individuals could set up foreign currency accounts which would be insulated from domestic accounts. An individual could export any goods including essentials that they obtained by redeeming their available money, and receive the foreign currency in their foreign currency account. If an individual wished to import something from a country that did not have a fixed-value currency relative to the domestic currency, and needed access to the foreign currency, someone else should have exported something of sufficient value in a foreign currency to be able to cover the imports. The importer could buy the foreign currency from the exporter by transferring domestic money from their domestic account to that of the seller. Any privately agreed-upon exchange rate would work, without upsetting the parity of Π with available surplus. The foreign currency would be transferable only between foreign currency accounts and these accounts could not hold domestic currency.

Domestic currency would not be transferred outside and foreign currencies would not enter the domestic market. If individuals holding foreign currency wished to convert it to the domestic currency, they could purchase bundles of essentials abroad, and then deposit these with the central store to obtain local currency. Foreigners selling in the local markets for local currency could use a commercial account like any other company. These accounts do not have periodic distribution associated with them. They could not transfer the money abroad directly. Instead they would need to obtain foreign currency in the same manner as importers, or export something to a foreign country to get the desired foreign currency from the sale made outside of the country.

A less restrictive system, one that allowed for the domestic currency to be held offshore, would also be possible. The central store could allow currency held in a domestic account to be transferred outside but would remove the equivalent goods and hold them in a separate foreign redemption account so that the currency held abroad would always be redeemable without any recomputation for available money. The goods would be removed from domestic available surplus calculations. The currency would be available to foreign holders without impacting domestic parity. Foreigners selling in the local market could then repatriate the available Π in their account to their home country. Exporters could also then get paid in domestic currency being held abroad. They could deposit such payments in their domestic account, and the central store would move back the corresponding surplus into its domestic account.

In other words it is always possible to work out the details to be able to maintain domestic parity, and if needed, keep any foreign holdings of the currency redeemable as well.

So if everything is so great, what are we waiting for? How do we convert our existing system to such a system? We do not go into this in any detail, and for good reason.

6.3 Starting towards the New System

To start the conversion of the system from an existing fiat-based system, on the goods side we can assume that governments would first build up two to three years of storage, which would take a while. The world does not currently produce sufficient surplus for this to be accomplished in a short period of time. Instead of diverting food from existing stocks, it may be better to work towards improving productivity and agricultural infra-structure, distribution systems as well as storage. These are actions governments need to take anyway, regardless of whether they wish to change over to a new currency system or not.

On the currency side the steps would involve conversion of the existing currency to digital form and providing each individual with a single account. Things are progressing towards a cashless society already. It would involve an orderly settlement of derivatives contracts and other such financial engineering innovations to remove them from the system, to be able to commence with the re-engineering. This would not necessarily be a bad thing and such settlements have already been considered when countries such as Greece were near default. As the final step banks would be nationalized, the shareholders paid the equivalent of their ownership, and loans would be moved to the central store account where they would contribute a negative amount to the total balance.

Once the total currency in the system is determined given all account balances, positive or negative, and the total surplus is known, the currency can simply be scaled so that one available unit of the new currency is equivalent to one unit of surplus available with the central store. Individuals would be free to open financial institutions in compliance with the new currency regime.

Clearly the task is a significant one, although even proceeding along the path has benefits. Our primary purpose, though, is not to get involved in detailed regulations and paths, of which there could be many depending on the preferences of the members of the system.

Our primary purpose is to demonstrate that changes in the fundamental paradigm of how we view the system can potentially lead to significant changes in system characteristics. In the context of careful evaluation of the underlying assumptions and formulations for internal consistency for social sciences, it is necessary to guard against what we would call *generally accepted* precepts, which represent gaps in perception as they are often taken to be axiomatic without much thought. Simple examples would be broad principles such as "demand goes down when price goes up," which does not hold during bubbles; or that "diversification can reduce risk," which may not hold during crises as individuals are forced to sell off unrelated assets to raise cash to cover positions in declining ones. Broader principles are also susceptible to such issues such as a system based on "democracy, free markets and liberty" where the first is one-person one-vote, the second is one-dollar one-vote, and the third is protection of individual rights regardless of wealth or majority opinion. General principles that have been used over centuries to explain phenomena have included both "like attracts like" and "opposites attract." If we keep trying to appease rain gods, the system may still go on, but there is no guarantee it will bring us any closer to desired results.

The analyses presented here suggest that a deeper discussion on the nature of currency may provide a fruitful and complementary area for policy consideration as compared to ever-more-complex mathematical modeling whose predictions are often not in consonance with realized outcomes. Similar issues may also hold for agent-based modeling which may simply shift the complexity to modeling of agent behavior. It is neither easy, nor desirable, to change system rules frequently in real-life human systems, which is why it is important to consider the rules carefully, without imposing overly restrictive assumptions on agent behavior.

Endnotes

1. Just to show that we are not simply making this up, Jervis (2012), Tetlock et al. (2012), Posner (2012), Jones-Rooy and Page (2012), and Friedman (2012) discuss the topic in a journal issue devoted primarily to this topic. Scientific papers on agent-based modeling also often refer to such issues. The discussion in Sargent (2014) may be of tangential interest as well.

2. See for instance Yilmaz and Dube (2014) for a dynamic estimation procedure for the estimation period, in the context of portfolio management strategies, that improves risk-adjusted performance.

3. In Dube and Dube (2013) we provide material modeling examples from engineering to demonstrate that even in physical sciences such issues are difficult to detect, and discuss how these issues can only be more severe for financial modeling. A model that requires variable parameters is incomplete, and reasonable-looking results from such a model do not imply the model is correct or that it has captured all significant factors.

4. See Goodkin (2012). The book title, *The Wrong Answer Faster: The Inside Story of Making the Machine that Trades Trillions*, is self-explanatory.

5. The textbook proof is in Copeland and Weston (1988).

6. Jaumotte and Buitron (2015) find that a major contributor to the rise in income at the top, along with the rise in inequality, is correlated to a decline in unionization.

7. Murphy (2014) suggests that it is unclear whether the less compassionate become wealthy or the wealthy are naturally less compassionate, but wealth and compassion typically do not go together.

8. At least if the sworn testimonies of CEOs of financial institu-

tions, after the financial crisis, are to be believed.

9. Olshansky et al. (2012) show significant disparities in life expectancy at birth between the highest-educated whites and the lowest-educated individuals of African descent. Even as race played a part, the life expectancy for white females with less than 12 years of education decreased from 1990 to 2008.

10. Newsmedia reports (Kolasa-Sikiaridi, 2016) state that the Monetary Policy Report 2015–2016 released by the Bank of Greece shows increased suicide rates, increased infant mortality by 50%, greater prevalence of mental illness, increasing from 3.3% in 2008 to 12.3% in 2013, and lack of affordable treatment increasing chronic diseases by 24%.

11. There are some studies that suggest that it is more economical to simply provide individuals with essentials rather than bear the costs of individuals not having access to these. See, for instance, Keyes (2014) which reports on one such study.

12. Gentilini (2014) compared 12 studies in 10 countries and noted that performance of cash versus in-kind assistance varies by indicators. For example, cash was more effective in enhancing food consumption while food seemed to outperform cash in increasing household caloric intake. Such debates are significant in India. The paper suggests the debate is "one of the most polarizing social protection quandaries" with strong opinions on both sides.

13. There is some evidence (see for instance Jhabvala, 2014) that schemes that do not have any means test are more effective towards attaining their objectives and that universal access schemes are more politically acceptable (Fondation Trudeau, 2013). Basic Income Guarantee schemes are being proposed and tested in various jurisdictions, and are even being endorsed by physicians (e.g. Adams et al., 2015) to avoid "toxic stress" from experience of poverty in early childhood

and as a form of "disaster insurance" to protect people from slipping into poverty given the employment issues. The most significant attempt has been in Switzerland, where it got sufficient signatures to be placed on a nationwide referendum. It did fail, but garnered more votes than even the originators had expected.

14. It is interesting that the references all predate the crash that followed the internet bubble.

15. Governments can typically decide upon such requirements in terms of basic components such as protein and calories, but converting it to cash equivalents can be somewhat more involved given regional variations in prices. See, for instance, Planning Commission (2014).

References

Acemoglu, D., Why Do New Technologies Complement Skills? Directed Technical Change and Wage Inequality, *Quarterly Journal of Economics* **CXIII** (1998) 1055–90.

Adams, R., et al., Letter from 194 Physicians to the Minister of Health and Long-Term Care, Toronto, Ontario (August 17, 2015). Accessed at https://d3n8a8pro7vhmx.cloudfront.net /bicn/pages/151/attachments/original/1439928444/Ontario_ph ysicians_letter_to_Hon__Eric_Hoskins_%28FINAL_August_ 17_2015%29.pdf

AFP, Indian officials order Coca-Cola plant to close for using too much water, *The Guardian* (June 18, 2014). Accessed at http://www.theguardian.com/environment/2014/jun/18/india n-officals-coca-cola-plant-water-mehdiganj

AFP, Richest 1pc of the world will have more money than the remaining 99pc by 2016: Oxfam, *South China Morning Post* (January 19, 2015). Accessed at http://www.scmp.com/news/ world/article/1681844/richest-1pc-world-will-have-more-money-remaining-99pc-2016-oxfam

Arnold, S., Market Democracy: Land of Opportunity?, *Critical Review: A Journal of Politics and Society* **26:3–4** (2014) 239–58.

Benes, J., and Kumhof, M., The Chicago Plan Revisited, *IMF Working Paper WP12/202, International Monetary Fund* (August 2012). Accessed at https://www.imf.org/external/pubs/ft/wp/ 2012/wp12202.pdf

Berg, A. G., and Ostry, J. D., Inequality and Unsustainable Growth: Two Sides of the Same Coin?, *IMF Staff Discussion Note 11/08, International Monetary Fund*, Washington (April 2011). Accessed at https://www.imf.org/external/pubs/ft/ sdn/2011/sdn1108.pdf

Berg, A. G., Ostry J. D., and Zettelmeyer, J., What Makes Growth Sustained?, *Journal of Development Economics* **98:2** (2012)

149–66. Working Papers (IMF, March 2008; European Bank for Reconstruction and Development, July 2011). Accessed at https://www.imf.org/external/pubs/ft/wp/2008/wp0859.pdf and http://www.ebrd.com/downloads/research/economics/workingpapers/wp0133.pdf respectively.

Bershidsky, L., What If Banks Didn't Create Money?, *Bloomberg View* (November 9, 2015). Accessed at http://www.bloombergview.com/articles/2015-11-09/what-if-swiss-banks-tried-100-percent-reserve-banking-

Bird, C., Why Not Marx?, *Critical Review: A Journal of Politics and Society* **26:3–4** (2014) 259–82.

Brede, M., Preferential Opponent Selection in Public Goods Games, *Advances in Complex Systems* **15:7** (2012) 1250074 (14 pages), DOI: 10.1142/S0219525912500749.

Bulut, E., Transformation of the Turkish Vocational Training System: Capitalization, Modularization and Learning unto Death, *Journal for Critical Education Policy Studies* **8:1** (2010) 362–88.

Caselli, F., Technological Revolutions, *American Economic Review* **89:1** (1999) 78–102.

Ceccobelli, M., Gitto, S., and Mancuso, P., ICT Capital and Labour Productivity Growth: A Non-parametric Analysis of 14 OECD Countries, *Telecommunications Policy* **36:4** (May 2012) 282–92.

Copeland, T. E., and Weston, J. F., *Financial Theory and Corporate Policy*, 3rd ed. (Addison Wesley, 1988).

Cravino, J., and Levchenko, A. A., The Distributional Consequences of Large Devaluations, *RSIE Discussion Paper 648* (November 2015).

Dobbs, R., Madgavkar, A., Barton, D., Labaye, E., Manyika, J., Roxburgh, C., Lund, S., and Madhav, S., The World at Work: Jobs, Pay, and Skills for 3.5 Billion People, *Report*, McKinsey Global Institute (June 2012).

Doms, M. E., Dunne, T., and Troske, K. R., Workers, Wages, and Technology, *Quarterly Journal of Economics* **112:1** (January 1997)

253–90.

Dube, M., and Dube, S., Criticality of Robustness Checks for Complex Simulations and Modeling, *Information Journal* **16:11** (November 2013) 7917–40.

Dube, S., Dube, M., and Turan, A., Information Technology in Turkey: Creating High-skill Jobs Along with More Unemployed Highly-educated Workers?, *Telecommunications Policy* **39:10** (November 2015) 811–20.

El-Erian, M. A., Does the US have a student loan problem? *World Economic Forum* (November 10, 2015). Accessed at https://www.weforum.org/agenda/2015/11/does-the-us-have-a-student-loan-problem

Elliot, L., Richest 62 people as wealthy as half of world's population, says Oxfam, *The Guardian* (January 18, 2016). Accessed at http://www.theguardian.com/business/2016/jan/18/richest-62-billionaires-wealthy-half-world-population-combined

Erb, C. B., and Harvey, C. R., The Golden Dilemma, *Financial Analysts Journal* **69:4** (July/August 2013) 10–42.

FAO, The State of Food Insecurity in the World, *Food and Agriculture Organization of the United Nations*, Rome (2015). Accessed at http://www.fao.org/3/a-i4646e.pdf

Fondation Trudeau, Responsible Citizenship: A National Survey of Canadians Commissioned by the Pierre Elliott Trudeau Foundation in Collaboration with Concordia University, *Trudeau Foundation and Concordia University* (October 31, 2013). Accessed at http://www.environicsinstitute.org/uploads/news/tf%202013%20survey%20backgrounder%20-%20responsible%20citizenship%20-%20oct%2031-2013%20eng.pdf

Forestier, E., Grace, J., and Kenny, C., Can Information and Communication Technologies Be Pro-Poor?, *Telecommunications Policy* **26:11** (December 2002) 623–46.

Frank, A., Could Automation Lead to Chronic Unemployment?

Andrew McAfee Sounds the Alarm, *Forbes* (July 19, 2012). Accessed at http://www.forbes.com/sites/singularity/2012/07 /19/could-automation-lead-to-chronic-unemployment-andrew-mcafee-sounds-the-alarm/#23e696323aa5

Friedman, J., System Effects and the Problem of Prediction, *Critical Review: A Journal of Politics and Society* **24:3** (2012) 291–312.

Gargiulo F., and Huet, D., New Discussions Challenge: The Organization of Societies, *Advances in Complex Systems* **15:7** (2012) 1250033 (17 pages), DOI: 10.1142/S0219525912500336.

Gentilini, U., Our Daily Bread: What Is the Evidence on Comparing Cash versus Food Transfers?, *Social Protection & Labor*, Discussion Paper No. 1420, World Bank Group (July 2014). Accessed at http://www.cmamforum.org/Pool/Reso urces/Cash-Vs-Food-Transfers.pdf

Goldin, C., and Katz, L. F., The Origins of Technology-Skill Complementarity, *Quarterly Journal of Economics* **113:3** (1998) 693–732.

Goldman, D., Worst year for jobs since '45: Annual loss biggest since end of World War II. Unemployment rate rises to 7.2%, *CNN Money* (January 9, 2009). Accessed at http://money. cnn.com/2009/01/09/news/economy/jobs_december/

Goodkin, M., *The Wrong Answer Faster: The Inside Story of Making the Machine that Trades Trillions* (Wiley, 2012).

Gourevitch, A., Welcome to the Dark Side: A Classical-Liberal Argument for Economic Democracy, *Critical Review: A Journal of Politics and Society* **26:3–4** (2014) 290–305.

Government of India, National Food Security Act (NFSA) 2013, Webpage, *Department of Food and Public Distribution*, Ministry of Consumer Affairs, Food and Public Distribution (2013). Accessed at http://dfpd.nic.in/nfsa-act.htm

Headlines Today Bureau, Foodgrains Rot in India's Godowns with No Space to Store, *India Today* (June 22, 2011). Accessed at http://indiatoday.intoday.in/story/foodgrains-rot-in-indiagodown-no-space-to-store-bumper-crop/1/142399.html

International Labor Organization, Global Employment Trends for Youth 2013: A generation at risk, *International Labor Office*, Geneva (2013). Accessed at http://www.ilo.org/wcmsp5/grou ps/public/—-dgreports/—-dcomm/documents/publication/ wcms_212423.pdf

Janssen, M. A., Manning, M., Udiani, O., The Effect of Social Preferences on the Evolution of Cooperation in Public Good Games, *Advances in Complex Systems* **17:3–4** (2014) 1450015 (22 pages), DOI: 10.1142/S 0219525914500155.

Jaumotte, F., and Buitron, C. O., Power from the People, *Finance & Development* **52:1**, International Monetary Fund (March 2015). Accessed at http://www.imf.org/external/pubs/ft/fandd /2015/03/jaumotte.htm

Jervis, R., System Effects Revisited, *Critical Review: A Journal of Politics and Society* **24:3** (2012) 393–415.

Jhabvala, R., No Conditions Apply, *Indian Express* (December 9, 2014). Accessed at http://indianexpress.com/article/opinion/ columns/no-conditions-apply/

Jones-Rooy, A., and Page, S. E., The Complexity of System Effects, *Critical Review: A Journal of Politics and Society* **24:3** (2012) 313–42.

Kampouridis, M., Chen, S.-H., Tsang, E., Microstructure Dynamics and Agent-Based Financial Markets: Can Dinosaurs Return?, *Advances in Complex Systems* **15:Suppl. No. 2** (2012) 1250060 (27 pages), DOI: 10.1142/S02195 25912500609.

Katz, L. F., and Murphy, K. M., Changes in Relative Wages, 1963–1987: Supply and Demand Factors, *Quarterly Journal of Economics* **107:1** (1992) 35–78.

Keyes, S., Leaving Homeless Person On the Streets: $31,065. Giving Them Housing: $10,051, *ThinkProgress* (May 27, 2014). Accessed at http://thinkprogress.org/economy/2014/05/27/3 441772/florida-homeless-financial-study/

Kitto, K., and Boschetti, F., Attitudes, Ideologies and Self-Organization: Information Load Minimization in Multi-Agent Decision Making, *Advances in Complex Systems* **16:2–3** (2013) 1350029 (37 pages), DOI: 10.1142/S021952591350029X.

Kolasa-Sikiaridi, K., Bank of Greece Report Concludes: "Greeks' Health Deteriorating, Life Expectancy Shrinks", *Greek Reporter* (June 17, 2016). Accessed at http://greece.greekreporter.com/ 2016/06/17/bank-of-greece-report-concludes-greeks-health-deteriorating-life-expectancy-shrinks/

Kuehn, D., Hayek's Business-Cycle Theory: Half Right, *Critical Review: A Journal of Politics and Society*, **25:3–4** (2013) 497–529, DOI: 10.1080/08913811.2013.853863.

Licklider, J. C. R., and Taylor, R. W., The Computer as a Communication Device, *Science and Technology* (April 1968). Reprinted in *In Memoriam: J. C. R. Licklider 1915–1990*, Digital Systems Research Center (August 7, 1990).

Mabry, R. H., and Sharplin, A. D., Does More Technology Create Unemployment?, *Cato Institute, Policy Analysis No. 68* (March 18, 1986).

Mehta, S., and Kalra, M., Information and Communication Technologies: A Bridge for Social Equity and Sustainable Development in India, *The International Information and Library Review* **38:3** (September 2006) 147–60.

Mincer, J., and Danninger, S., Technology, Unemployment, and Inflation, *NBER Working Paper Series, No. 7817* (July 2000). Accessed at http://www.nber.org/papers/w7817

Mogilner, C., The Pursuit of Happiness: Time, Money, and Social Connection, *Psychological Science* **21:9** (August 2010) 1348–54.

Mokyr, J., *The Lever of Riches: Technological Creativity and Economic Progress* (Oxford University Press, 1990).

Murphy, J. B., Free Market Morals, *Critical Review: A Journal of Politics and Society* **26:3–4** (2014) 348–61.

OECD, Focus on Inequality and Growth: Does Income Inequality Hurt Economic Growth? (December 2014). Accessed at http://www.oecd.org/els/soc/Focus-Inequality-and-Growth-2014.pdf

Olshansky, S. J., et al., Differences in Life Expectancy Due to Race and Educational Differences Are Widening, and Many May Not Catch Up, *Health Affairs* **31:8** (August 2012) 1803–13.

Planning Commission, Report of the Expert Group to Review the Methodology for Measurement of Poverty, *Government of India* (June 2014). Accessed at http://planningcommission.nic.in/reports/genrep/pov_rep0707.pdf

Posner, R. A., Jervis on Complexity Theory, *Critical Review: A Journal of Politics and Society* **24:3** (2012) 367–73.

PTI, Inequality increasing in India says International Monetary Fund, *Financial Express*, Washington (February 5, 2014). Accessed at http://www.financialexpress.com/news/inequality-increasing-in-india-says-imfs-christine-lagarde/1223005

Rahman, S. A., 2.3 Million Apply for 368 Office Jobs in Indian State Government, *Voice of America* (September 18, 2015). Accessed at http://www.voanews.com/content/indian-state-government-swamped-with-applications-for-peon-job/2968912.html

Sargent, T. S., The Evolution of Monetary Policy Rules, *Journal of Economic Dynamics & Control* **49** (2014) 147–50.

Sassi, S., and Goaied, M., Financial Development, ICT Diffusion and Economic Growth: Lessons from MENA Region, *Telecommunications Policy* **37:4–5** (May–June 2013) 252–61.

Schweitzer, F., Mavrodiev, P., and Tessone, C. J., How Can Social Herding Enhance Cooperation?, *Advances in Complex Systems* **16:4–5** (2013) 1350017 (22 pages), DOI: 10.1142/S0219525913500173.

Sieniuc, K., Canadian schools ease standards to draw more foreign students, *Globe and Mail* (August 12, 2014). Accessed at http://www.theglobeandmail.com/news/national/education/schools-fast-tracking-foreign-students-to-offset-declining-enrolment/article20023502/

Singh, A., Have you bought or earned your PhD? *Careers 360* (January 6, 2014). Accessed at http://www.university.care ers360.com/articles/have-you-bought-or-earned-your-phd

Son, H., We've Hit Peak Human and an Algorithm Wants Your Job. Now What?, *Bloomberg* (June 8, 2016). Accessed at http://www.bloomberg.com/news/articles/2016-06-08/wall-street-has-hit-peak-human-and-an-algorithm-wants-your-job

Sukhtankar, S., *Corruption and the Mahatma Gandhi National Rural Employment Guarantee Act* (July 16, 2012). Accessed at http://www.ideasforindia.in/Article.aspx?article_id=1#sthash. VnNXXsQJ.dpuf

Tetlock, P. E., Horowitz, M. C., and Herrmann, R., Should "Systems Thinkers" Accept the Limits on Political Forecasting or Push the Limits?, *Critical Review: A Journal of Politics and Society* **24:3** (2012) 375–91.

The Gazette of India, The National Food Security Ordinance, 2013, No. 7 of 2013, The Ministry of Law and Justice (July 5, 2013). Accessed at http://www.prsindia.org/uploads/media/ Ordinances/Food%20Security%20Ordinance%202013.pdf

Upbin, B., The 147 Companies that Control Everything, *Forbes* (October 22, 2011). Accessed at http://www.forbes.com/sites/ bruceupbin/2011/10/22/the-147-companies-that-control-everything/

USDA, Supplemental Nutrition Assistance Program: National View Summary, *Food and Nutrition Service* (2015). Accessed at http://www.fns.usda.gov/sites/default/files/pd/34SNAPmont hly.pdf

Woodyard, C., Exxon Mobil CEO: No fracking near my backyard, *USA Today* (February 22, 2014). Accessed at http://www.usa today.com/story/money/business/2014/02/22/exxon-mobil-tillerson-ceo-fracking/5726603/

World Bank Group, *Food Price Watch*, Year 5 Issue 17 (May 2014).

Yilmaz, T., and Dube, S., Asset Allocation and Stock Selection: Evidence from Static and Dynamic Strategies in Turkish

Markets, *Iktisat Isletme ve Finans* **29:344** (November 2014) 73–94.

Yukalov, V. I., and Sornette, D., Self-Organization in Complex Systems as Decision Making, *Advances in Complex Systems* **17:3–4** (2014) 1450016 (30 pages), DOI: 10.1142/S021952591 4500167.

BOOKS

Iff Books

ACADEMIC AND SPECIALIST

Iff Books publishes non-fiction. It aims to work with authors and titles that augment our understanding of the human condition, society and civilisation, and the world or universe in which we live.
If you have enjoyed this book, why not tell other readers by posting a review on your preferred book site. Recent bestsellers from Iff Books are:

Why Materialism Is Baloney
How True Skeptics Know There Is No Death and Fathom Answers to Life, the Universe, and Everything
Bernardo Kastrup
A hard-nosed, logical, and skeptic non-materialist metaphysics, according to which the body is in mind, not mind in the body.
Paperback: 978-1-78279-362-5 ebook: 978-1-78279-361-8

The Fall
Steve Taylor
The Fall discusses human achievement versus the issues of war, patriarchy and social inequality.
Paperback: 978-1-90504-720-8 ebook: 978-184694-633-2

Brief Peeks Beyond
Critical Essays on Metaphysics, Neuroscience, Free Will,
Skepticism and Culture
Bernardo Kastrup
An incisive, original, compelling alternative to current
mainstream cultural views and assumptions.
Paperback: 978-1-78535-018-4 ebook: 978-1-78535-019-1

Framespotting
Changing How You Look at Things Changes How
You See Them
Laurence & Alison Matthews
A punchy, upbeat guide to framespotting. Spot deceptions and
hidden assumptions; swap growth for growing up. See and be
free.
Paperback: 978-1-78279-689-3 ebook: 978-1-78279-822-4

Is There an Afterlife?
David Fontana
Is there an Afterlife? If so what is it like? How do Western ideas
of the afterlife compare with Eastern? David Fontana presents
the historical and contemporary evidence for survival of
physical death.
Paperback: 978-1-90381-690-5

Nothing Matters
A Book About Nothing
Ronald Green
Thinking about Nothing opens the world to everything by
illuminating new angles to old problems and stimulating new
ways of thinking.
Paperback: 978-1-84694-707-0 ebook: 978-1-78099-016-3

Panpsychism
The Philosophy of the Sensuous Cosmos
Peter Ells
Are free will and mind chimeras? This book, anti-materialistic
but respecting science, answers: No! Mind is foundational to all
existence.
Paperback: 978-1-84694-505-2 ebook: 978-1-78099-018-7

Punk Science
Inside the Mind of God
Manjir Samanta-Laughton
Many have experienced unexplainable phenomena; God,
psychic abilities, extraordinary healing and angelic encounters.
Can cutting-edge science actually explain phenomena
previously thought of as 'paranormal'?
Paperback: 978-1-90504-793-2

The Vagabond Spirit of Poetry
Edward Clarke
Spend time with the wisest poets of the modern age and of the
past, and let Edward Clarke remind you of the importance of
poetry in our industrialized world.
Paperback: 978-1-78279-370-0 ebook: 978-1-78279-369-4

Readers of ebooks can buy or view any of these bestsellers by clicking on the live link in the title. Most titles are published in paperback and as an ebook. Paperbacks are available in traditional bookshops. Both print and ebook formats are available online.

Find more titles and sign up to our readers' newsletter at http://www.johnhuntpublishing.com/non-fiction

Follow us on Facebook at
https://www.facebook.com/JHPNonFiction
and Twitter at https://twitter.com/JHPNonFiction